CLASSIC CARS

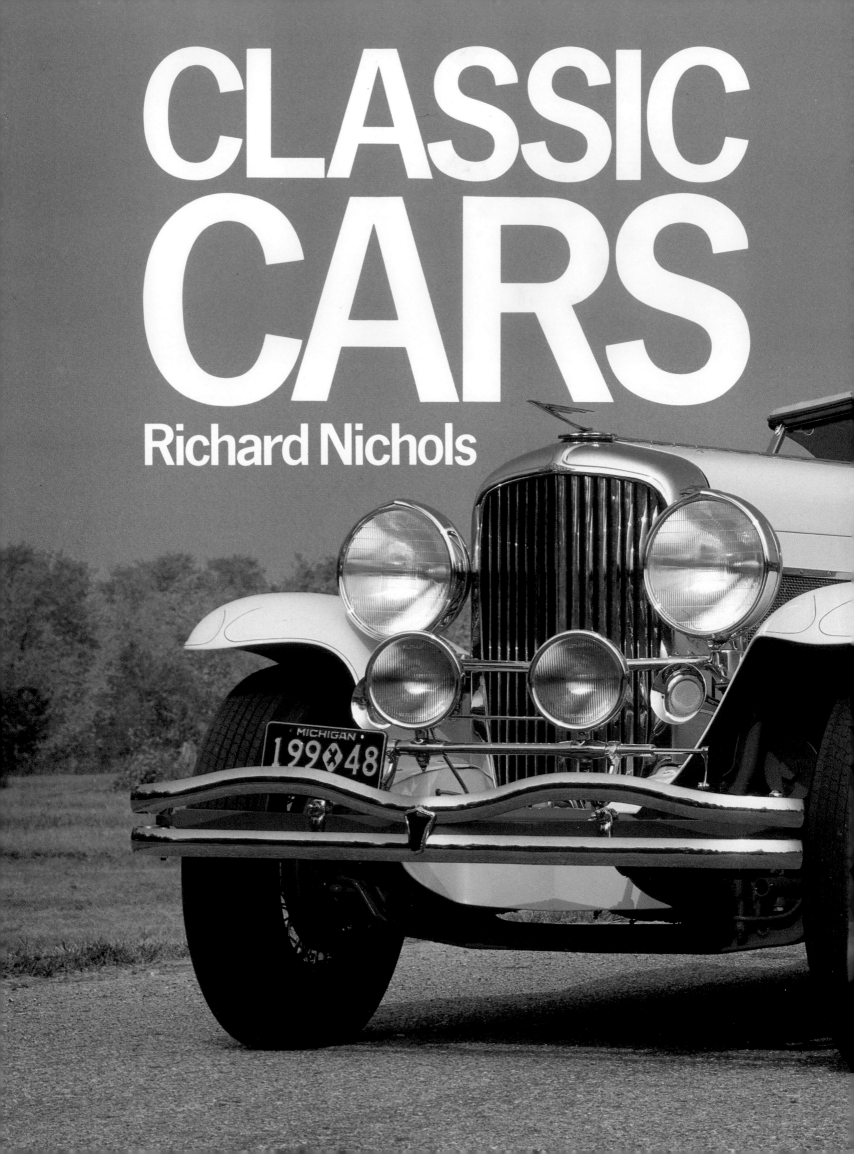

CLASSIC CARS

Richard Nichols

BISON GROUP

First published in 1993 by
Bison Books Ltd
Kimbolton House
117A Fulham Road
London SW3 6RL

ISBN 1-85841-018-5

Printed in Hong Kong

Page 1: Spiritual successor to the fabled SS-100, the Jaguar XK 120 was
introduced in 1948 and by 1959 had become this XK 150, last of the range
before the advent of the XKE.
Pages 2-3: Originally built in 1933, this supercharged Duesenberg SJ boat-tail
coupe was rebodied in the late thirties by Waltham.
Below: Classic, good-looking, rare and expensive, the 1936 Cord 810
Westchester.

Contents

Aston Martin

The Aston Martin name was established at the beginning of the 1914 war, largely as a result of Lionel Martin's hillclimb success in modified Singer sportscars. The name was drawn from a combination of Martin's own and from the Aston Clinton hillclimb venue, and existed for several years before the first real Aston Martin car was built. This was still based on the Singer but was intended to be an improvement, faster, smoother and easier to drive. Real competition involvement began around 1920 but the marque was better-known for its drivers, like Count Zbowski, than it was for race success. Then in 1922 Aston Martin entered the first Grand Prix, which was not a resounding success. But in the same years the car began to collect world records in endurance and speed trials at Brooklands and things started to look up.

However, throughout its life the company was to be beset with financial problems which were never truly resolved for very long. It was saved from collapse the first time by a syndicate which included ace mechanic Augustus Bertelli, under whose guidance the future brightened, and Aston Martin had class wins at Le Mans in 1932 and 34, and a second place in 1933. Almost all of the company's vehicle production was two-seat sportscars although there were occasional saloons throughout the thirties. After World War II the company continued with the development of a prewar Claude Hill design, named the Atom, but by 1947, as financial problems loomed, it was still not beyond the experimental stage. It was then that David Brown took the company over, and the added finance speeded development of the Atom so much that it was ready for launch within a year, and went on sale in 1948 as the Aston Martin DB1. Only a tiny handful of these four-cylinder, 2-liter cars were made in the ensuing two years, despite a win at the Spa 24 Hours in 1948. Good-looking enough, fast enough, the DB1 was outrageously expensive when compared to its major rival, the Jaguar XK120, and in any case the existing

Above: Originally designated the Atom, the first postwar Aston Martin was renamed the DB1 after the company was taken over by David Brown. Above right: Engine detail from the 1959 DB 2/4. Below: The DB2 from 1950.

Above: Restyled by Mulliner as the DB2/4, this is the Mk III version with the larger engine and slightly altered nose.

Left: The familiar-shaped DB5.
Below left: The first of the Aston Martin supercars, the V8 Vantage.

Right: Breathtaking good looks plus incredible electronic sophistication, the Aston Martin Lagonda. Below: the most familiar Aston Martin of them all is almost certainly the 007 car made for the James Bond film *Goldfinger*.

facilities at the Aston Martin factory in Feltham, west London, were totally inadequate for production of any real volume.

In 1950 the DB1 was replaced by the DB2, a car which used the same chassis layout as the DB1 but which had a six-cylinder dohc engine of 2.5 liters which had been designed for Lagonda by W O Bentley. Lagonda was yet another ailing car company bought into the David Brown empire, which had been founded on the manufacture of tractors. Early development of the DB2 led to a complete chassis rebuild and on top of that was added new 2 + 2 bodywork by Mulliner; this car was designated DB2/4 and was the familiar forerunner of the rest of the now-famous DB series. It remained in production for a considerable period and was given a major facelift in 1957 when the DB2 Mk III was introduced – a DB2 with a bigger, 3-liter engine and a restyled nose.

The DB2 was considered an excellent car, and would have continued to be popular had Aston Martin kept it in produc-

tion. But by now the factory had moved to larger premises at Newport Pagnell and a considerable volume of cars was being produced; the DB2 in its various guises was in production for nine years and almost 1800 of them were built until it was replaced by the DB4.

This was an altogether sharper-looking car which was tending towards the same luxury GT market occupied by marques like Ferrari, and continued development of the Lagonda straight six allowed its performance to keep pace with developments made by competitors who perhaps learnt more from their considerable race involvement. By the time the DB5 was introduced the six-cylinder engine was a 3.6-liter unit and by 1964 it had grown to a massive 4.0 liters producing a more than adequate 282bhp, making the DB5 a very fast tourer indeed. It was this powerplant which was fitted to the DB6, but it was a V8 engine which was destined to place Aston Martin very firmly in the supercar league.

A capacity of 5.3 liters, dohc per bank of cylinders, a power output which Aston Martin refused to quantify in terms other than 'adequate' and a top speed of around 145mph is good enough for any car to be accepted as a first-class contender. But the high-compression version of that same engine which was fitted into the Aston Martin Vantage was even better than that. The output of the Vantage engine is also undisclosed by Aston Martin but probably lies somewhere between 400 and 450bhp. Whatever it is, it's enough to give the car – still a luxury four-seater of considerable weight – a top speed marginally in excess of 170mph, where only exotic types like the Ferrari 365 Daytona or the Lamborghini Miura are fast enough to keep up.

It is this engine which is also fitted to the electronically surfeited Aston Martin Lagonda to produce a rare combination of speed, comfort and technical wizardry at a price which ensures owners almost total exclusivity, as well as to the Nimrod and Bulldog, which are perhaps esoterica rather than exoticars.

Auburn-Cord -Duesenberg

Erret Lobban Cord was a self-made millionaire before he was 30 and was sufficiently well-respected to be called in to aid the failing Auburn company in 1926. Auburn–Cord swiftly moved in on the equally shaky Duesenberg company and, along the way, made the far more advantageous purchase of the Lycoming engine factory. Under Cord's guidance the combine began to prosper. In fact they did well enough to survive the 1929 crash, which was no mean achievement for a company whose products were markedly

at the luxury end of a market tending toward economy products.

In the main this was due to Cord's tough leadership and his own capacity for innovation. The Cord became an automobile made in limited numbers and sought after out of all proportion to its original worth. It incorporated a number of revolutionary features, not least of which were the wraparound gills which replaced the traditional upright radiator grille, front wheel drive and independent front suspension (both had been done before, but not combined on one car) and retractable headlamps, which Cord copied from aircraft landing lights.

The ACD products were intended only for those who could afford the very best — the Auburn 'boat-tail' Speedster sold for more than $15,000 in the early thirties as a chassis only, at a time when Henry Ford's replacement for the Model T, the Model A, was selling complete for a mere $385. It was designed as an extravagant car for an extravagant market, meant to demonstrate to anyone who saw it that the owner had not only survived the Great Depression but had emerged unscathed from a financial disaster which had wrecked the previously booming American economy in a comprehensive fashion.

The Speedster had been designed by one part of a combine which enjoyed individual reputations for the construction of superb cars. The Cord 810 'Coffin-nose', the one with all the refinements and innovations, established a unique reputation almost the day it was announced, and Duesenberg had long been recognized as a name of quality engineer-

Above: 1932 Auburn 12 – 161A V12 Sedan. Right: 1936 Auburn 852 Supercharged Convertible Cabriolet.

Above: 1935 Auburn 851 Phaeton Sedan.

Above and above left: The 1937 Cord 812 Supercharged Phaeton, not only dramatic in appearance but technically ahead of its time.

Left: The 1936 810 Westchester Sedan, while undeniably goodlooking, lacks the visual impact of the more glamorous Phaeton.

ing by all who knew the automobile world. The Auburn was also a very special make of car. The 851 Speedster set up a record which lasted for a great many years when, at the hands of Ab Jenkins, 'the Mormon Meteor', it had streaked non-stop across the Bonneville salt flats, covering 1200 miles in 12 hours; that's a constant speed of 100mph for 12 hours. The Speedster had a straight eight engine, equipped with an already-developed Duesenberg supercharger, and was offered for general sale in that trim. Each production model of the 851 Speedster bore a dash plaque stating that it has been individually tested at 100mph before delivery.

Design of the Speedster is attributed to either Gordon Buehrig or Count Alexis de Sakhnoffsky; sources differ as to which individual (if it was not a joint project) was responsible for its looks. Thanks to the collapse of the Auburn–Cord–Duesenberg empire in the thirties, it is unlikely that the whole truth will ever become known. That the Speedster was a truly beautiful motorcar is indisputable though; but it is a great shame that it arrived too late to save the combine from disaster. It was available as a slightly cheaper option, minus supercharger and chromed convoluted headers, but even then its sales were insufficient to keep it alive.

Fortunately it did not completely disappear in the way of the coffin-nose Cord, of which precious few examples survive today. By virtue of his purchase of the Lycoming factory, Cord's personal empire did not vanish with ACD, and the factory found great financial success as a manufacturer of aero engines; Lycoming-built units were fitted

Left: 1935 Duesenberg JN Berlina by Rollston.

Below: 1935 Duesenberg SJ Roadster bodied by Gurney Nutting of London. Bottom: First built in 1929, this Duesenberg J was rebuilt in about 1937 by Graber of Switzerland.

to many World War II fighter aircraft, Mustangs and Spitfires in particular. This continuity ensured that at least some parts of the car manufacturing process survived, and the original Auburn molds are still in existence.

The Auburn–Cord company revived the car in the late seventies, using those molds, and began a limited production of glassfiber Auburn Speedsters based on the big Lincoln chassis with some strengthening and using a big-block Ford V8 of 427ci capacity. Although made in glassfiber the car can hardly be called a replica, since it does have inch-for-inch accuracy and authenticity, coming from those original molds. They're not inexpensive, but then they're not as expensive as original Cords, and they have survived a production gap of almost 50 years. And, however you look at them, they're still excessively opulent, excessively good-looking and excessively expensive. In fact, they're still selling to exactly the same sector of the market as did the originals when they were introduced all those years ago.

Bentley

Walter Owen Bentley was widely known as 'W O'. After he left college he became a railway apprentice, but winning a gold medal in the 1907 London to Edinburgh reliability trial changed all that, and he decided that his future would be not with trains but with the newly-popular motorcar, and he formed a company with his brother 'H M', importing French cars, DFP, Buchet and La Licorne. Almost at once he began racing, with a DFP, and had started record-breaking attempts when the outbreak of war in 1914 brought an end to that sort of thing. When the war was over he formed the Bentley Car Company which continued more or less where he'd left off, with a primary interest in motor racing, although by the time the company was taken over by Rolls-Royce in 1931 its products were clearly of a fairly high and luxurious standard, racing success or not.

Racing success was what W O was after and where he achieved fame, however, and for a considerable number of years it was the Bentley cars which upheld the British flag on the racetrack, and it was his 'Bentley Boys' who were

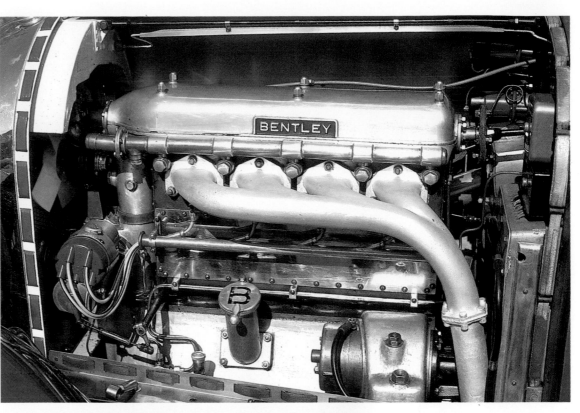

Above left: The big Bentley 3-liter probably the example of the marque which is best remembered. Above: Engine detail of the 3-liter.

Left: The 6.5-liter was suitably imposing in appearance.

Left: The fearsome-looking 6.5-liter coupe.

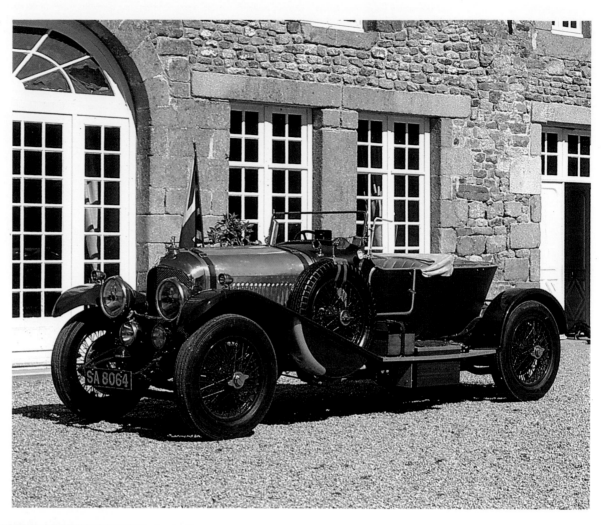

Below left: A 1930 8-liter sports saloon by Mulliner. Right and above right: The 3-liter model with engine detail.

responsible for so much of his success. In fact it was a lone Bentley which represented Britain at the very first *24 heures du Mans*, one of W O's new 3-liter cars, driven by Duff and Clement. Perhaps it was the total absence of any front-wheel braking system whatever which enabled the Bentley to establish the very first Le Mans lap record, 67mph, in a race which an incredible 30 of the 33 starters survived and finished, the Chenard et Walcker of Lagache/Leonard covering 1372 miles.

In 1924 the same Bentley returned to Le Mans, this time with brakes on all four wheels, again the sole British representative out of a field of 40, the other cars all being French. This time it emerged as the victor, the first of a series of Bentley wins at Le Mans and the first hint that the prewar history of the race would be largely dominated by the car and the Bentley Boys. However that was not immediate, and the following two Le Mans races were won by Lorraine

Dietrich, but the Bentley was back in 1927, this time with a stablemate, the new 4.5-liter. The bigger car crashed at White House corner and the faithful 3-liter carried the flag again, crossing the finish line in first place. But the following year was a triumph for the bigger car, and the 4.5-liter took a third Le Mans title for Bentley, although even that was but a preparation for the truly vintage year of 1929.

A 6.5-liter Bentley had been built since 1925, a six-cylinder vehicle of impressive dimensions and carrying capacity and in 1929 this engine was built into a convertible sportscar destined to be a classic of its era. The Bentley Speed Six was built in the days before sportscars had to be small, streamlined and handy. Traditionally shaped, it bore an imposing countenance and brought 180bhp out of its 6.5 liters at 3500rpm. The sound made by that lazy engine as each of its six massive pistons thump up and down is unmistakeable even today. Unsurprisingly the Bentley Boys, as they were by now known, appeared with the car at Le Mans.

Their reputation and nickname preceded them, their exploits were already famous. In 1927 the 3-liter of 'Sammy' Davis and Dr Benjafield had been involved in a six-car accident at the White House corner which had put paid to the big 4.5-liter car, but Davis extracted the smaller Bentley from the wreckage and drove on to win. This year of 1929 saw the full team of the Bentley Boys ready for the fray, and they were a mixed bunch. Davis was a journalist, Benjafield a medical doctor, George Duller a jockey and Jack Dundee a theatrical impresario. The team was backed by the money of the Hon. Dorothy Paget and Captain Woolf 'Babe' Barnato, the latter taking an active part in the team's exploits as well, sharing his drive with Sir Henry 'Tim' Birkin.

It was the big six of this latter pair which led the field

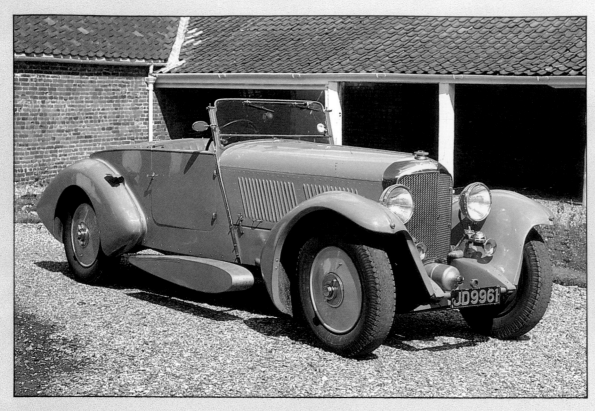

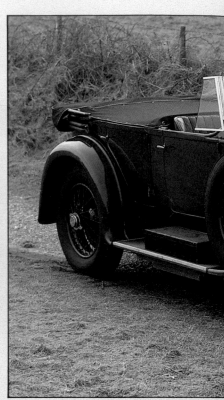

Above right and below: A 1931 8-liter Sports Tourer. Above: Front view of the 6.5-liter boat-tail.

across the finishing line of the 1929 24 Hours, followed by a procession of Bentleys as the 'Boys' scooped first, second, third and fourth places — the whole team had survived, with no other car in front of them. They repeated their success the following year, fending off the challenge of the 7-liter Mercedes team led by Caracciola, Babe Barnato taking the flag once again in his third successive win at Le Mans. And although that was the last of the Bentley era, the 'Boys' won again the following year, 'Tim' Birkin and Lord Howe collecting the honors in an Alfa Romeo.

The Bentleys were gone, though, the successor to the Speed Six being a monster 8-liter, 220bhp vehicle on an entirely new chassis which arrived on the market just in time to take a sound drubbing, not from a competitor but from the gloom of the Depression. Financial problems became worse, and in 1931 Rolls-Royce bought the company, marketing their own vehicles under the prestigious Bentley name.

Bentley, himself, moved on to Lagonda in 1935, the year they won Le Mans with a Meadows-engined 4.5-liter car, later redesigned by W O for greater comfort and luxury. Almost his last act before retirement was to design for Lagonda the big V12 engine and the 2.5-liter V6 which powered postwar Aston Martins.

Bugatti

Although the cars were made in France, and Bugatti is always recognized as a French make, Ettore Bugatti was, as the name suggests, Italian, and despite lengthy residence in France he remained an Italian citizen until very shortly before his death in 1947. His interest in motorcars began in 1898 when he purchased a petrol-engined tricycle, and shortly afterward he commenced work as an apprentice in a Milanese machine-shop. Less than a year later he had built his own tricycle, and it won eight out of the ten races he entered with it. Thus encouraged, in 1902 he left Milan to work for De Dietrich in Alsace, which was then German territory. Almost at once he began to build cars in his own name, and in 1911 a Bugatti finished second in the French Grand Prix, marking the beginning of an era of unparalleled success which lasted until the outbreak of the Second World War. In 1925 and 1926, years somewhat better than average it must be admitted, Bugattis won 1045 different events, scored another 806 in 1927, enjoyed five successive Targa Florio victories and seemed to be at every race event winning every trophy.

The vehicle which led up to this domination, and which had supported the company virtually singlehanded before then was the Brescia. It was primarily based on the Type 13, a small competition car built for sprints and hill climbs in 1910. The Brescia went into production after the end of the Great War, during which time Bugatti himself had been working on aero engines which were produced in America by the Duesenberg factory.

Right: A Type 57 Ventoux, introduced in 1934. Below: A Type 37A Grand Prix from 1927. Below right: The famous Brescia Bugatti, mainstay of the company between 1918 and 1922.

It was a four-cylinder, 1368cc, 40bhp engine with an overhead camshaft which powered the Brescia, with the peculiar Bugatti curved tappets operating four valves in each cylinder. The Type 13, postwar version, was Bugatti's only model until the introduction of the Type 30, a straight eight, in 1922, and took the first four places at the Italian Voiturette Grand Prix at Brescia in 1921, from which it then took its name.

It was available on several different chassis, and the shorter racing cars were known as Full Brescia while the bigger touring cars were, properly, Brescias Modifiés. Like most cars of the time, braking was a rear-wheel-only affair, at least until British racer Raymond Mays, who cam-

The Bugatti Type 57SC. Left: Driver's view through the cockpit and across the long hood. Below: The supercharged 3.3-liter engine. Bottom: The famous horseshoe Bugatti radiator cowl.

Below right: From 1923, the Cadillac Series 63 Coupe.

paigned Brescias for the champagne-makers Mumm, fitted front brakes to his car, a practice soon followed by other Brescia racers. The car continued in production until 1926, by which time about 2000 of them had been made, a few under license in Britain, Germany and Italy, the only Bugatti of which this is true.

Bugatti also made fast saloons and tourers which are counted among the finest ever, and were certainly sold to crowned heads and aspiring members of society and many of the best examples were built during the thirties. Aside from the more exotic examples of the marque, the Type 57 stands out as an elegant touring saloon, with its sharply-raked windshield and full-fendered lines, and was also the last Bugatti to go into series production.

Introduced in 1934, the Type 57 was Bugatti's attempt to produce a fast and economical sedan which was cheap enough to be considered as everyday transport. Its straight eight, dohc engine produced some 135bhp out of 3.3 liters, 160bhp when supercharged as the 57C. Even so le Patron, Ettore Bugatti, deemed syncromesh a luxury and still clung to mechanical brakes even though hydraulics were replacing them on just about every other vehicle being manufactured at the time, certainly in the type of market the Type 57 was aimed at. In fact hydraulic brakes were not adopted until 1938, by which time the days of the Bugatti were numbered anyway.

By 1939 the Type 57 was the fastest saloon which could be bought as stock, and because of the collapse of the French franc in 1936 it was a remarkably inexpensive car in other countries, selling for less than £900 in Britain. About 700 of the Type 57 were built before the war, but it failed to take off again afterwards in revamped guise as the Type 101. In any case there were other problems. Bugatti's factory had been commandeered during World War II and when it was over he was forced to go to court to win it back, being forced to prove that he, Ettore Bugatti, was the owner of the Bugatti factory at Molsheim. He won his case, of course, but died in his sleep the same night.

Cadillac

Henry Ford and Henry Leland terminated their partnership at the end of 1902. Ford went on to become Ford, and Leland went on to become Lincoln, although that wasn't for a long time. To begin with Leland reorganized the company Henry Ford left behind and named it Cadillac after the founder of Detroit, Antoine Cadillac. Their first production car was a Henry Ford design, reworked by engineer Leland to make its single-cylinder engine as reliable and efficient as possible. A mere 14 years later Cadillac introduced their first V8 and have kept it as their basic engine ever since.

They pioneered electric starting and electric lighting on their cars, and were so sure of the reliability of the new system that they supplied their vehicles without a starting handle, and blanked off the hole in which it would normally be fitted. Cadillac swiftly gained a reputation for such reliability and longevity, and their cars were highly prized and sought after; rising and established members of the infant and influential Dream Factory springing up in the orange groves of California began to be seen in Cadillacs, although Packard remained America's number one prestige vehicle.

High standards of production, together with a yet unknown standardization of parts, had been Cadillac's first major contribution to the motor industry. In 1909, the same year in which Cadillac became part of the then tiny General Motors Corporation, three of their four-cylinder Model 30 cars had been completely stripped and reassembled into three different but perfectly functional vehicles after all the parts had been thoroughly mixed up. This had won Cadillac their first Dewar Trophy and was the beginning of their famous slogan, 'Standard of the World'.

Cadillac benefited greatly from the talents of GM stylist Harley Earl, and later from Bill Mitchell, both of whom later rose to the heights of a combine which would soon be making 50 percent of the cars produced in America. It was the stylist Earl who recognized the importance of the styling factor and started Cadillac, and the US auto industry as a whole, on the pattern of seasonal styling changes.

Cadillac emerged from the '29 Crash in a fairly strong position, and along with Cord's Auburn–Cord–Duesenberg setup, recognized the need for luxury sedans again at the beginning of the thirties. To meet this need the company introduced what is probably one of the American auto industry's all-time classic vehicles, the V16 Sedan de Ville.

The engine was designed by Ernest Seaholm, a narrow 45-degree cast iron V16 of 7.4 liters (454ci). It featured updraft carburetors, dual headers, hydraulic tappets, overhead valves and produced 165bhp at a sedate 3400rpm.

It was super-quiet and silky-smooth, representing ultimate luxury. The open body was traditionally styled, without the futuristic appearance of the Cord progeny. Huge lamps sat between the upright grille and flowing outboard fenders, and a squarish body by Cadillac's exclusive coachbuilders, Fleetwood, sat on a lengthy (148-inch) chassis.

No less than 3863 V16 cars were built between 1931 and 1938, all of them bodied by Fleetwood, all of them the best that Cadillac could offer. And while Cord's empire strangled and died, Cadillac flourished. This was mainly due to their support from the rapidly-growing GM, also to the fact that,

Right: 1931 Series 452 V16 Sedanca de Ville, rebodied by its British owner as a Town Car. Below: 1931 Cadillac V16 Type 452 Cabriolet.

unlike most of the independents, they offered a wide choice besides their top-of-the-range limousines. Cadillac, like Packard and others, introduced 'economy' models, although the former branded theirs separately, as LaSalle, wisely retaining the exclusivity of the Cadillac name for the luxury sedans, an oversight which would eventually cost the Packard company its life.

In 1938 Cadillac ceased production of Seaholm's engine,

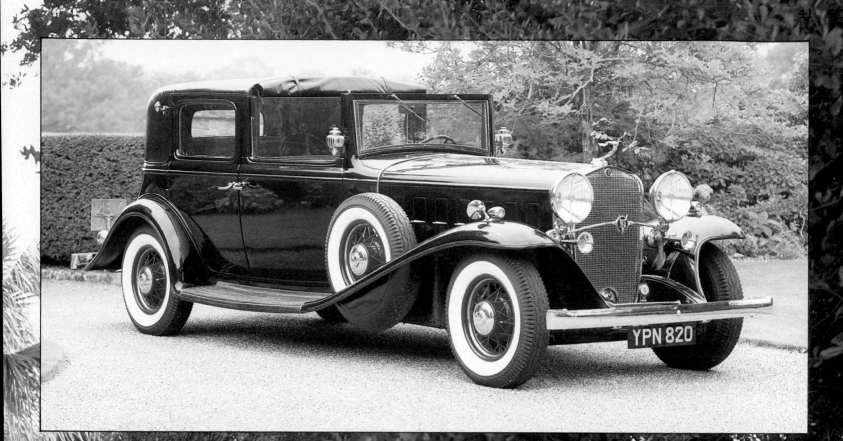

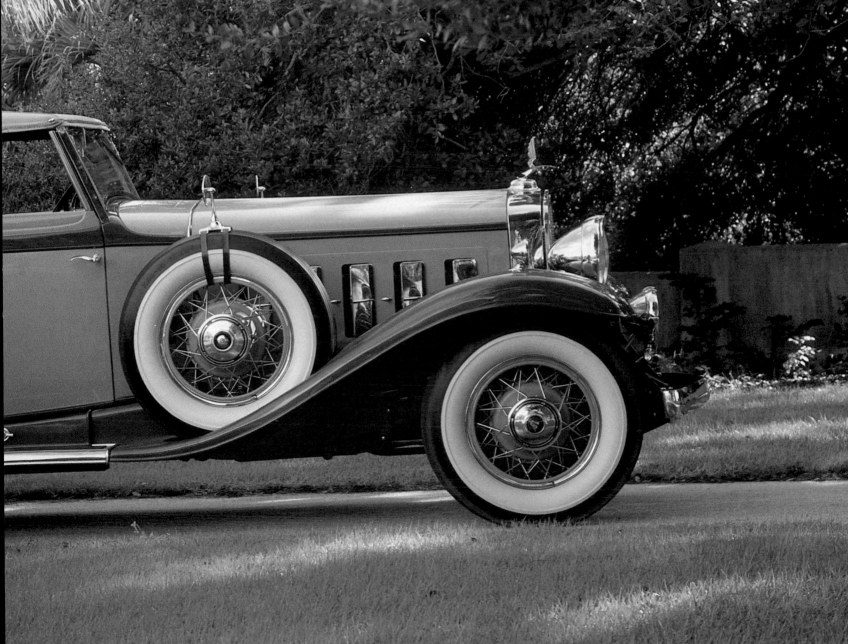

although the V16 continued as they introduced an L-head version which was considered by most to be inferior. Even though the era of the V16 may well have been reaching its end in any case, the sidevalve surely hastened it; a mere 511 were built between 1938 and 1941, and the monster engine disappeared forever.

The sidevalve was more powerful than its predecessor, producing 185bhp out of a 431ci cast iron 135-degree V16. It ran nine main bearings, had dual distributors and, like Ford's V8 introduced in 1932, had separate water pump and cooling for each bank of cylinders. Only 61 of the big V16 cars were built in 1940, which was its last year of production, by which time it was clear that a time of austerity was on the way and that passenger car production as a whole would have to cease anyway. By this time the V16 was being fitted into a Series 90 five-seat sedan which bore no resemblance whatever to the elegant cars of the thirties and which would never attain the classic status of its graceful forerunners.

Top and above left: 1939 Series 60 Sedan in side and front view, showing the distinctive grille arrangement. Left: A 1940 Town Car with coachwork by Brunn.

Right: 1956 Chevrolet Bel Air two-door hardtop.

Chevrolet

Louis Chevrolet had been making cars for years. As early as 1927 he had swept Henry Ford off the top slot as the most productive motor manufacturer in the USA, but in the period after World War II the market seemed to swing the other way. Mostly this was due to the fact that other manufacturers, and Ford in particular, had bounced back after the war with a series of up-to-date designs. Improvements in engineering technology which had been accelerated by the war were freely available but somehow Chevrolet seemed slow to bring them onto the production line, and the early fifties Chevrolet models were a rather lumpy and sluggish competitor to the sleeker and more powerful Fords. The Ford flathead V8 had been available to the public since the Model B of 1932 and was *the* performance option, even without Zora Arkus Duntov's 'Ardun' hemi-head conversion, which doubled its power. Chevrolet were still clinging to the old 'stovebolt' straight six and losing out quite markedly.

In 1955 all of that changed, and Chevrolet fortunes took a distinct turn upwards. So much improvement was ushered in during 1955 that Chevrolet saloons introduced that year and refined through until 1957 are now considered to be the company's classic products — the Tri-Chevys. In fact the new models were so popular that the

Left and below: Widely agreed on as *the* classic from the Tri-Chevy years, the '57 Bel Air Convertible.

first production year saw 1.7 million units sold — and that in the 'slabbiest' of the classic years — and more than six million altogether over the three-year run. Part of their success was inevitably due to their new powerplant which replaced the old straight six — Chevrolet's first V8 for more than 30 years. This was the 265ci smallblock which had materialized just in time to save Corvette from the accountants' red pen and put the '55 Chevrolet sedans on a more than equal footing with their competitors from Dearborn, although Ford were still outselling them.

The '55 model was carried on into '56 and, instead of getting a new look for '57, received only a facelift in a year in which Chrysler introduced their rather stylish new designs from the drawing-board of Virgil Exner. But in the process fans of the classic Chevrolet were given what was to become the all-time favorite, the debonair '57. Altogether

lighter in appearance than the '55, the facelift models had a stylish grace which the '55 had entirely lacked and it was hard to believe that they were in fact the same car. All the paneling seemed lifted by the pronounced sweep of the tail fins and a wraparound toothy chrome grille which owed much to Ferrari's Superamerica. As the pillarless Bel Air coupe and the soft-top convertible the '57 Chevrolet was a styling exercise of supreme elegance.

However, the reworking was not confined to cosmetic changes, and the new models featured many under-the-skin changes of great importance. The most significant addition was the new-generation smallblock V8, uprated to 283ci and considerably more powerful than before, mated to a new automatic transmission, Turboglide, available for the first time. The 265 was still available, as was the 'Blue Flame' version of the straight six, giving the sedans for 1957 a

range of different engine options which extended from 162 to 283bhp. All the attention went naturally to the 283bhp, 283ci smallblock, since it represented something of a milestone; one bhp for each cubic inch of displacement. Coupled with the Turboglide automatic gearbox, which had the luxury of a kickdown for the first time, and which was only available with the 283 motor, the new cars were the fastest Chevrolet had ever made, moving from rest to 60mph in 10 seconds.

The new cars were launched in October 1956, offering 19 different body styles from the 150 Sedan through 210 and Bel Air, and although they still didn't outstrip Ford in that year they did sell a comfortable 1.5 million vehicles. They were unquestionably the best and most advanced sedans the company had so far offered, and were marketed on the basis that everyone who wanted a Cadillac but couldn't afford one would buy a Chevrolet instead. It was a philosophy which worked very well. Although the '57 didn't have the splendidly tasteless bodywork of the big Cadillacs they had something which was rather understated but expensive-looking nonetheless.

Along the way they also became the most desirable sedans Chevrolet ever produced and earned a rightful place in the collectors' market; thousands of them survive today, but in spite of their availability a good condition '57 is still worth a considerable sum of money.

Top: The 1958 Chevrolet Biscayne. Although the three classic years are properly over by '58, it is still a good-looking and much-prized collectors' car. Above and below: Still much the same as it was at its introduction in 1953, this Corvette hardtop is from 1955, the last year in which the original body style was retained.

Corvette

Beyond any doubt the Chevrolet stand was the centerpiece of the 1953 New York Autorama. Star of the stand was a white experimental two-seater designated EX 122, which generated such enthusiasm and interest from the visitors who queued for hours just to look at it that it went into production, and the first glassfiber Corvette rolled off the Flint production line just six months later, on 30 June.

Originally the glassfiber was intended as a temporary measure until suitable tooling to make the bodies in steel could be arranged, but it was so successful that it was retained, even though the first cars were built from 62 separate panels hung round a fairly traditional frame and suspension, although the low-slung engine was much further back than was considered usual. This layout had been arranged by a young Cal Tech engineering graduate, Robert McLean, was approved by the instigator of the project and the principal stylist, the legendary Harley Earl (who is said to have influenced the appearance of more than fifty million automobiles in his thirty-year working life) and pushed into production by Chevrolet's dynamic Ed Cole.

At the time of its introduction it was a revolutionary enough vehicle, especially for Chevrolet. The company had been making cars since 1911 and had dominated the marketplace since 1927, when Louis Chevrolet pushed Ford off top slot, apparently for all time. For a company dedicated to the mass market, the production of a low-volume sportscar was something of an oddity, and when poor sales continued for two years it seemed likely that the whole Corvette project would be axed. But then Ford entered the arena with their new 'personal car', the Thunderbird, and Corvette was kept alive to compete against it.

Left alone it probably would have gradually faded away. Mechanically it was far from revolutionary, was noticeably underpowered, and had little appeal to sportscar buyers. But in 1955 Zora Arkus Duntov, a Belgian-born Russian engineer working for Chevrolet, began to take a hand in Corvette production and gradually stamped it so heavily with his own personality and expertise that it is almost universally regarded as 'his' project.

Duntov's first major task was to give Corvette the sort of performance which a sportscar should be capable of. It had started life with Chevrolet's 'stovebolt' straight six which was good for about 150bhp out of 235ci displacement. By 1955 it had acquired Chevrolet's first V8 for years, a 265 with 195bhp and a top speed of about 118mph installed in Corvette, and after considerable work on the steering —

which he improved no end — Duntov turned to the engine. The 1957 Corvettes were fitted with a 283ci V8 which produced the ideal and previously unattainable figure of 283bhp; one horsepower for each cubic inch of displacement.

Duntov's own-design camshaft was produced for the enthusiast, and became the single most essential performance

Top: The 1961 Corvette convertible was much sleeker than its predecessors, and the tail shape and the line over the rear fenders would remain much the same for the next 20 years. Left: The famous split rear screen featured for one year only on the all-new for 1963 Sting Ray. Below and below right: Dashboard detail and interior of the 1958 model.

item for the smallblock V8 for the next decade. With the acquisition of real power the smallblock rapidly became the most desirable and most easily-tuned engine around, almost certainly the most popular performance engine ever. And it did now perform. The '57 Corvette was capable of 133mph; later versions, especially the fuel-injected 327ci, were capable of phenomenal speeds, and some Corvettes available from the factory were good for about 180mph.

The body style, changed in 1955, went through several minor variations before the next major alteration and the production, in 1963, of one of the world's motoring legends — the Sting Ray. Flatter, sleeker and altogether more aggres-

Above: The 1968 Corvette, with waisted body, pointed droop-snoot and removeable T-top roof panels.

sive than previous models, the Sting Ray looked as though it was traveling at 150mph all the time, even when it was parked. Equipped with Duntov's new independent rear suspension in place of the traditional solid back axle, Corvette could now handle all the horsepower it had been equipped with, and the irritating skipping at the rear end was gone.

In this guise Corvette was a winner in every sense of the word and was ready to deal with the racetrack threat posed by Shelby's Ford-powered Cobra. But the Chevrolet racing program was canceled before the confrontation took place, and so it was five unofficial entries which appeared at the Nassau Speed Week in late 1963, where French journalist Bernard Cahier observed that it was 'immensely powerful, but controllable', and said that its performance and handling were 'well ahead' of both the Ferrari GTO and the Cobra. His subjective opinion was entirely borne out by the results of the racing. Chevy power swept the board and Corvette won just about everything with the possible exception, said Spence Murray, of the Ladies' Cup and the Grand Prix of Volkswagens.

From then on Corvette went from strength to strength. Thanks to Duntov's persistence it acquired disk brakes which are still among the most smooth and powerful available on any automobile in the world. So good are they

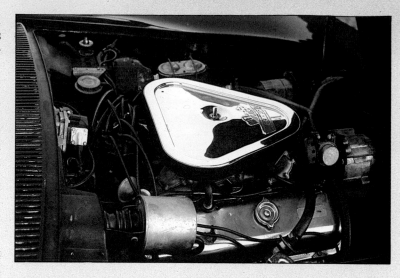

at hauling the car down from 100mph-plus test stops – on an endless basis – that Chevrolet reported to the SAE that the braking potential of the system was 'limitless'. *Road and Track* magazine found them so good that they became bored waiting for something to happen during high-speed test stops.

Now suitably engineered, Corvette was given its most powerful engine packages ever. In 1965 it was available

Above: Engine detail from the 1969 model. Below: This 1966 Corvette is one of the best-looking and most dramatically styled examples of a series which has specialized in dramatic appearance for 30 years.

with a 427ci powerplant which was rated at 425bhp and gave top speeds around 150mph. By 1967 the L88 aluminum-head version was introduced; 560bhp and a potential 170mph. The ultimate was the aluminum ZL-1, intended as a race engine and producing 585bhp, all based on the Can Am race cars of the McLaren team.

As 1968 came and went Corvette changed its style to the smoothly curved shape with pointed snout and sharply cut off tail. With only the addition of the body-color polyurethane nose and tail this style remained in production from '68 through '82 — half of the vehicle's production life. In that period it indelibly stamped the swoopy curves and the narrow waist on the minds of all sportscar enthusiasts and managed to retain the essence of the performance road car even though the fuel crises of the early seventies and the growing environmental lobby gradually robbed Corvette of its power. Even though by 1975 there were only two low-compression 350ci versions of the famous smallblock available to Corvette buyers, even though neither of them was good for more than 200bhp, Corvette still looked like a performance car, still looked like a legend.

In 1978 the Corvette celebrated 25 years in production. It had by now ceased to be regarded as a model from the Chevrolet factory; although parts interchange is high, Corvette is a make of car in its own right and carries no Chevrolet or GM badges anywhere on its coachwork. Only a number in its serial number identifies its Chevrolet origins. And in 1983, an incredible 30 years after its introduction, Corvette went through yet another styling change, getting a new, flatter, almost European shape as well as a new independent rear suspension, aluminum suspension components front and rear and various other technical innovations. Rumors about the long-awaited restyle had included a mid-mounted engine and a rotary engine. Up front on the all-new for '83 models, though, is still the smallblock V8; thirty years after *its* introduction, it's still in high demand, just like Corvette.

Top and above: Details of the 1978 Corvette Limited Edition (main picture below), brought out to celebrate 25 years of Corvette production. Right: All new for 1983, the long awaited restyle ironed out the swoopy curves and gave Corvette an almost European look.

De Tomaso Pantera

Allessandro De Tomaso is really Alejandro of the same name, son of an Argentinian politician, a leading rebel against Juan Peron and thus something of an exile. His motor racing career began in Argentina but was carried on in Italy while he worked as a mechanic at Maserati during the fifties. He formed De Tomaso Automobili in 1960 and his first projects were pure racing cars for Formula Two and later Formula One. His sole entry in F1 was in 1970, with a car driven by Piers Courage, Brian Redman and Tim Schenken, but he retired the team midway through the season after they had finished in only two races.

Although his success with De Tomaso sportscars using a variety of European engines was reasonably encouraging, in the mid-sixties he decided that he would use Ford engines exclusively, after his successes with the small British engines from the Anglia and Cortina, and he applied this principle when he decided to build GT cars for road use. The first project, the Vallelunga, was Cortina-powered, and had a glassfiber body built by Ghia (which he had acquired along with Vignale, Benelli, Moto Guzzi and Maserati). There are no production records for Vallelunga, and the car was never actively marketed in America, but probably between 50 and 100 of them were made. In any case De Tomaso felt that it was underpowered, and that a bigger engine was needed. To this end he was looking to Ford in America to provide the same sort of performance as Shelby's Cobras.

The prototype of the next model, Mangusta, was revealed at Turin in 1966. Its 43-inch tall body was designed by Giugiaro, then at Ghia, made in fiberglass, powered by an aluminum engine which was a De Tomaso replica of Ford's 302 Windsor and reputedly of more than 500bhp. By the time it made production the aluminum engine was replaced by the stock iron motor and the fiberglass body was now built in steel and aluminum. But it was a performer and a true GT car, of which 401 models were built between 1966 and 1971.

It was succeeded by the Pantera, which was a project aided by the liaison between De Tomaso and Ford, although all design and development work was done in Italy. Ford's expertise was drawn on in the area of mass production, something which De Tomaso was not very good at. In fact there were several areas which left room for complaint on the Mangusta, but De Tomaso was not interested in complaint. Criticized for the lack of front bumpers and somewhat inadequate windshield wipers he simply observed that the car had been built to be driven, not parked, and it shouldn't be driven in the rain.

This rather slapdash attitude of half-completed projects and rapidly changing enthusiasms characterized the entire factory output in the early days and perhaps accounted for the lack of success in Formula One. Certainly it landed Ford with problems once cars developed under the new partnership began to sell in the USA through Ford's Lincoln–Mercury Division. Perhaps developed is the wrong word, since De Tomaso had missed out on a great deal of the preproduction development and research which normally irons out so many irritating faults, and left Ford to pick up the pieces and make repairs, sometimes literally, by the roadside.

The Pantera of 1973, two years after its introduction,

Left and center left: Introduced in 1966, the De Tomaso Mangusta was styled by Giugiaro and powered by Ford.

Below and bottom left: The Pantera succeeded the Mangusta in 1971. This is the later GTS.

was so different to the original that it was designated L, and the improved version at this stage was a tribute to Ford and the patience of De Tomaso customers, for factory efforts were now directed toward the Group 3 and Group 4 racers, the latter having a claimed 570bhp output. Somewhere along the way Ford became fed up with the entire situation and bought their way out of the partnership, leaving De Tomaso Automobili to De Tomaso, but taking with them Ghia and Vignale. They closed Vignale, but retained Ghia as their own Italian styling house.

De Tomaso kept Maserati and the motorcycle outfits and continued to build Panteras at a slow pace, although once

again there are no real records to show the number of cars built. But as the price escalated, the car was emasculated: the 351 Cleveland engine finished its life and was replaced by the 302 and the supercar era drew slowly to a close. But somehow, out of all the apparent confusion and disorganization, De Tomaso Panteras have become as legendary as they are rare; their performance is more than adequate, road-holding neutral and secure, looks stunning and reliability excellent. The mid-mounted engine is, after all a Ford, if it breaks down in the middle of nowhere then any mechanic can fix it, once he's been shown where it is, which is more than you could expect with Ferrari or Lamborghini.

Facel Vega

The Facel Vega, introduced in 1954, represented several major firsts. It was, aside from anything else, a first for Jean Daninos and his company, Forges et Ateliers de Construction d'Eure et de Loire, from whose initials the name Facel comes. Founded before the outbreak of the 1939 war, Facel originally produced tools and dies for the aircraft industry, later expanding to deal with anything requiring their pressing technique, knowledge and equipment. This clearly included bodies for motorcars, and by the early fifties Facel was supplying complete bodies to Panhard, Simca and Ford France. When Panhard canceled production of their Dyna-Panhard, Daninos was left with a large amount of spare capacity at his plant which he chose to fill by making his own car.

Although pressed metal makes up a large proportion of the car, and he was equipped to cope with most other things, the major area in which he was helpless was of course the engine. Before the war a great number of small specialist manufacturers had overcome this problem by buying engines from the big corporations, so his decision to follow suit was not in itself altogether new. But Daninos chose to buy from America, where only a tiny few had purchased their powerplants before him. The combination of his own body-chassis unit with a big Chrysler V8 was so successful that it was soon followed by others; Jensen and Bristol in Britain, De Tomaso in Italy are perhaps the best known. It was a short cut to the supercar status which Ferrari and others had bought expensively, developing their own V8 or V12 engines from hard-won racetrack development.

The bodywork for the car was styled in-house, by Daninos and his design team, and surprisingly was no ugly duckling. It may look somewhat slabby and cumbersome today, but it was unusual and elegant by the standards of its time. This body was welded directly to a tubular chassis during construction, and the car had independent coil-spring suspension at the front and a live axle on semi-elliptic leaf springs at the rear. It was, a trifle unusual for the period, a 2 + 2, the luxury GT format which is now the accepted supercar configuration, and it was a large and heavy vehicle, at 15 feet long, six wide and just over 4000lbs in weight.

But that was no problem for the big V8 engines, and the Vega had an impressive specification sheet, with a top speed around 140mph and a 0-60 time of just over eight seconds. Originally the engine was the 4.5-liter Dodge hemi, but in 1959 the Vega was revamped, and became the Facel Vega HK 500. Body styling altered but little, the drum brakes were dropped in favor of disks and the V8 became the 6.2-liter which would also find a home in Britain's Jensen Interceptor. Two years later the HK 500 was itself restyled to become Facel II, a completely different-looking car with much smoother and sleeker bodywork which, with a slightly more powerful version of the Chrysler V8, gave it a top speed in excess of 150mph.

Production was slow, but demand was never anticipated as being especially high; the Vega was a large expensive car which could be expected to have limited appeal to a small number of wealthy people. Production ceased in 1964 and by that time the car had been through three variants; perhaps no more than 1000 units in total were built during that time, and certainly less than 200 Facel IIs ever saw the light of day.

What brought about the closure of the Facel production line was not the big luxury cars but, surprisingly, Daninos' attempt to go into volume production of a small car. The Facellia was introduced in 1959, looking like a scaled-down version of the Vega. In this case, however, he opted against an imported or even a domestic proprietary engine and a 1.6-liter dohc straight four was designed, and manufacture was entrusted to Pont-à-Mousson, who were already building gearboxes for the Vega.

However the Facellia, although cheaper than the staggeringly expensive Vega — which cost more than Aston Martin, Maserati or Ferrari — was still expensive compared to its rivals. Worse still, the new engine was a disaster. Designed by Carlo Marchetti, who had worked successfully for Talbot for years, it burned pistons with frightening regularity, and it was two years before the cause of the problem — in the cooling system — had been identified and eradicated. By the time that had happened it was too late, and the market for Facellia was non-existent. In four years only slightly more than 1000 were sold, which was hardly better than the big Vegas. The twin-cam engine was abandoned, and in 1963 Facel III was fitted with powerplant by Volvo — early twin-cams were being recalled for this engine to be transplanted; but it was all too late. Facel could not carry the financial burden imposed by the total failure of the Facellia range and in 1964 the company went into liquidation.

Right: The Vega, first car to be made by Facel themselves (after they stopped pressing bodies for Panhard) with any real success.

Below: The Facel Commette, from 1952, lacked the sophistication and big-car luxury of the Vega.

Lusso and the 250 GTS California were both better looking and better appointed. But somehow it was the GTO which took all the admiration.

Straightforward roadgoing cars which were part of the 250 series began with the Europa, in 1953, but the 250 GT didn't appear until 1956, with the 3-liter V12 and coachwork by Pininfarina. It stayed in production until 1960, by which time almost 500 examples had been built, and there were a few changes during the period. Most significant was Ferrari's adoption of disk brakes, a step he had been reluctant to take, even on race cars, for some time.

When the 250 GT was phased out it was replaced by a 2+2, the first sign from the factory that concessions could be made to the family motorist who still required performance. Inevitably this led gradually to the development of the luxurious high-performance road cars which are still civilized enough for everyday use and for which Ferrari is now more famous than for anything else other than Grand Prix racing. The first of these was the 250 GT Lusso (which means luxury) and was probably the first Ferrari in which two people could hold a conversation while traveling at any appreciable speed. The bodywork was a mixture of 250 GTO and 250 GT by Pininfarina and the car was a classic in every sense.

The 275 series followed, and they were the first GT cars with independent rear suspension, but even bigger changes were due, since Ferrari had by now recognized that the mid-engine configuration was clearly the most effective. It was already being used on the racetrack and was forming a successful partnership with the Forghieri-designed flat 12 engine in the 312 PB after various combinations of rear-mounted V12 layout had been tried in the 275 P and the 330 P with some considerable success. The flat, or boxer (hence the B in the Ferrari designation) 12 was taken from the Formula One circuits to power the sportscars and gave the 312 PB a top speed of some 200mph out of its 3-liter capacity.

It was at this point that the Ferrari team withdrew from sportscar racing to concentrate on Formula One, and the heritage of the 250 series was carried on by the road cars alone, leading to the production of some of the finest GT cars ever seen on the road. The 365 series appeared in 1968 with much of its design and appointments dictated by the American market and the increasingly stringent safety and exhaust emission regulations. It was a luxury 2+2 with a 4.4-liter engine, power steering and air conditioning and truly elegant coachwork. Before it appeared on the market, which was some three years later, the 365 GTC was already something of a legend, but the final pinnacle of achievement appeared as the 365 GTB/4, which was christened the Daytona even before it was announced at the Paris Salon of 1968.

It was powered by the 4.4-liter, 4 ohc V12 and produced 350bhp, giving it a top speed in excess of 170mph, possibly the highest genuine top speed of any road-going car. On top of the engineering was a Pininfarina body which must rank as one of the masterpieces of a styling house which was already recognized for excellence and expertise. If anything, removal of the slim-pillared roof to produce the spyder version, of which several were made to customer order, improved the flowing elegance of the coupe's shape, but whichever way you prefer it, the Daytona has to rank as the best GT car ever made, even though it is front engined and current practice allows that the mid-engined layout is superior.

It was succeeded, in 1973, by the 365 GT/BB, which looked far more like the two-seat sports Ferrari than the Daytona had. Nevertheless it was never as popular as the Daytona, lacking the classic grace of its predeccessor although it was just as fast and, thanks to its mid-engine location, handled rather better. It was replaced in 1976 by the 512 BB, which retained the flat 12 of the 365 GT/BB but with slightly increased capacity, at 4942cc and in appearance differed only in minor detail.

Above: The few 365 GTB/4 spyder conversions are, if anything, even more attractive than their factory-specified hardtop counterparts.
Left: Designated Lusso (meaning luxury) the 250 GTL Berlinetta was superbly appointed as well as superb-looking.

Below: The 365 GTC/4, introduced at the Paris Salon of 1971, some three years after the appearance of the GTB.

Ford Thunderbird

Henry Ford's first job had been with Con Edison where he had been working with electric lighting. In his spare time he'd built himself a car, and followed it with a second, much improved version which he felt was good enough to go into production. His first venture, the Detroit Automobile Company failed when Henry Ford was 38. He continued motor racing, however, and attracted enough attention to form the Henry Ford Company to build cars. Policy disagreements led him to resign, and the company was reconstituted by Henry Leland as the Cadillac Automobile Company. Henry Ford, in 1903, formed the Ford Motor Company in Detroit, buying parts from outside and assembling them into motor cars. In late 1908 Ford launched the Model T, assuring the company its success and the auto industry a legend. He was 45.

Two wars later, after the death of his son Edsel, Henry Ford passed over control of his company to Henry Ford II, who would stay in control through a period of great success, retiring in 1980. Unlike his grandfather, Henry Ford II was receptive to progress and advance, encouraged development and actively sought the employment of the most talented engineers and executives he could find. Under his leadership Ford developed an aggressive marketing policy which kept it locked in a grim struggle with General Motors as each sought to outdo the other.

However, GM's introduction of the Corvette in 1953 was not the spur which produced the Thunderbird; a two-seat sports convertible had been on the drawing-board for some while since market surveys had identified the need for such a car at the very turn of the decade. Indeed, Ford took much

greater account of such surveys than did GM, and it was information gained from such research which led to the change in policy over Thunderbird after it had been in production for only a few years. Two-seaters planned for the 1958 model year were canceled as a result, and the Thunderbird became a four-seat 'personal car' in which luxury was emphasized rather more strongly than sportiness; as a result Thunderbird outsold Corvette by a fairly wide margin, although it never gained the place in legend which the still-extant Corvette has earned. But the early two-seaters and the later convertibles were vehicles of considerable elegance and turn heads to this day.

Introduced in 1955, the Thunderbird cost around $3000 without options and was powered by the Y-block 292ci V8. Right from the start it was a big car, at 15 feet long, came with manual or automatic transmission, optional hardtop and gave 193bhp. By the following year it had grown to 202bhp and, as an attempt to increase trunk space, carried the spare tire outside the trunk lid; the T-birds with this 'continental kit' remain among the most desirable examples of the marque. The hardtop also came with optional portholes behind the side window, and as porthole versions far outsold the others almost all '57 Thunderbirds had that hardtop option fitted.

The two-seat Thunderbirds were given a facelift in 1957, as slight tailfins and a combined front bumper and grille were added but this was the last year of the two-seater. The four-seat Thunderbird appeared in 1958, a squarish rather slabby vehicle on a 113inch wheelbase, but with plenty of room for four. The importance and accuracy of market research was evident as the '58 outsold the '57 by more than double, and the '59 and '60 models were only slightly different in detail to the original design for a four-seat personal car.

The 1961 models were completely new, far sleeker with none of the slabbiness which had characterized the 1958–60 cars, and came with a 390 V8 of 300bhp, as a hardtop or roadster. In 1963 the policy was reversed and the four-seater was offered as a two-seater, the Sports Roadster, but production was limited; it cost a great deal more than the

four-seat convertible, and the tonneau cover was extra to that. Less than 2000 were made over a two-year production run, making these attractive vehicles the rarest of the T-bird breed.

The 1964 restyle squared up Thunderbird again, losing the embryonic tailfins and flattening the pointed front end into a wraparound combination far more reminiscent of the '58 models. This was the last of the classic looks, which remained in production until 1966. During its run the car came with disk brakes, swing steering wheel for driver access, 'cockpit' passenger compartment, 'silent-Flo' ventilation, sequential turn signal and a power-operated convertible top which stowed itself in the trunk at the press of a switch.

From 1966 onwards Thunderbird became little more than a faintly sporty-looking sedan, but as most sedans of the period aimed for that sporty appearance it distinguished itself hardly at all. Indeed, many purists will argue that, with the exception of the Sports Roadster, only the '55, '56 and '57 model years are collectable in any way at all.

Above: Tail view of the '56 Thunderbird with the Continental Kit for spare tire carriage. Right: The classic '57 with hardtop and porthole window.

Below: By 1963 Ford's 'personal car' has grown in response to market research and now sports four seats. This 1963 model has the rare fiberglass tonneau which converts it back into a two-seater.

Jaguar

In 1922 when William Walmsley, who had been making motorcycle sidecars in Stockport, Cheshire, moved to Blackpool he met William Lyons and together they formed the Swallow Sidecar Company, producing sidecars of unusual elegance. Their business prospered and in 1926 they added to their repertoire, beginning to build car bodies, fitting them mostly to the Austin 7 chassis to begin with, and later to the Morris Cowley. In 1927 the company changed its name, becoming the Swallow Sidecar and Coachbuilding Company as the volume and profitability of motorcars began to far exceed that of the original sidecar. In order to exploit this even further the company moved from Blackpool to Coventry and began making cars on a much larger scale.

With the move came the first car they could truly call their own. Although the SS1 was based on a Standard-built chassis and engine they had both been made specially for the SS, which was a low, swooping saloon of unusual good looks and staggeringly low price – £300 for SS1 and a mere £200 for its smaller counterpart, SS2. In 1934 the company was renamed again, this time becoming SS Cars Ltd, and it was they who gained the benefit of Harry Weslake's skill when he designed an overhead valve conversion for the Standard engine giving it vastly increased power. The SS90, so called because 90mph was its quoted top speed, was a sportscar of some grandeur, but the true classic to emerge from this pre-war period was the SS100, a rakish sportster easily capable of 100mph and blessed with classic lines by William Lyons, who had developed the same flair for styling as Walmsley had exhibited in his first motorcycle sidecars.

As the war ended the company changed its name again; although SS cars had a reputation the initials by now had a more unfortunate connotation, and so Jaguar Cars Ltd was born. Although they had been engaged, like all motor manufacturers, on war work, Jaguar had still managed to continue development, planning for the day war ended. Like all manufacturers there are apocryphal tales of how the Chairman of the Board, the Chief Designer and the Gatekeeper sat on the roof during bombing raids and designed their entire postwar range on cigarette packets. Someone must have done it, but whether it was William Lyons designing Jaguars or Alec Issigonis designing the Morris Minor will probably never be known.

What is true is that very soon after the war the new

Right: The 3.5 liter SS Drophead of 1937.

Below: The car for which the prewar SS company gained so much acclaim, the truly stunning SS100.

Above: Michelotti built this rare and unusual body for an XKE in 1963.

Right: This is the XKE which Phil Hill raced in the 1963 24 Heures du Mans.

Jaguar range appeared borne along by an entirely new engine which was so smooth, flexible and powerful that it was destined to remain in use into the forseeable future and beyond. Designed by Claude Baily, Bill Heynes and Walter Hassan, it benefitted, as had the prewar SS cars, from the combustion expertise of Harry Weslake, who gave it a light alloy cylinder head carrying dual cams, with angled valves set in a hemi-head combustion chamber. Carburation was by dual SUs and the six-cylinder 3.4-liter engine produced 160bhp.

This powerplant was destined to become standard to Jaguar saloons for decades, but William Lyons felt that there should be a sportscar and most of the design for the XK120 was his. The short chassis was a fairly standard box-frame arrangement, front suspension was independent torsion bar and the solid rear axle was carried on leaf springs. Steering was by recirculating ball, it had vast 12-inch drum brakes and a four-speed manual transmission.

Its bodywork was the thing, though. Low, curved and exciting, it created a sensation in 1948 when it was announced, a sensation which doubled when the full potential of the engine was realized. Stripped of hood and windshield, an XK120 was timed over the flying mile at 132mph; it had a speed and performance superior to most big American V8 engines and would retain that supremacy for many years, taking several Le Mans wins from its 3442cc.

And as if that wasn't enough, the car was inexpensive as well, selling for £1200 in Britain and $4000 in America. In fact it was so popular as an export vehicle that fewer than 10 percent of XK120 production was fitted with right-hand drive for the domestic market, the bulk of production going straight overseas.

In 1951 the open XK120 was joined by a fixed head which was even better-looking than the roadster, and in 1954 it was replaced altogether by the XK140, a 190bhp car with other improvements, including rack-and-pinion steering and better brakes. By now the impact of the styling was beginning to wear off and the copycats — Healey, MGA etc — were starting to appear. The XK140 was superseded by the heavier and coarser XK150, and later by the XKE, based on the racing C and D types.

Lamborghini

The money, the factory and the engineering/production knowledge existed well before 1964 when the Miura, a mid-engined V12, was announced. Lamborghini had been building tractors for some while, a few miles down the road from Maranello, and he decided that it was possible to build better cars than Ferrari, so the Miura was born. Lamborghini had several attempts with front-engined sportscars before Gian Paolo Dallara produced the transverse-engined Miura in spyder form in 1964. The V12 engine had four overhead cams, six 2bbl carburetors, four liters and 350bhp. With a five-speed transmission in unit, slung at the rear of a monocoque body on a box frame, it zapped the 2700-lb Lamborghini straight into the supercar bracket at 170mph, right alongside Ferrari. Within a few years the Miura had been fitted with three 3bbl carburetors and now produced 385bhp, giving it a top speed of 180mph. The Miura remained in production for nine years, and about 900 of them were built before the series was replaced.

This time the V12 was rear-mounted longitudinally with the transmission bolted to the front, so that it protruded forwards between the seats. The bodywork was by Bertone and the car was named Countach, which is an Italian expression of immense surprise and amazement, which seems fitting. The styling was dramatic at the very least. The doors opened forwards and upwards from hinges in the front of their frame — not gullwing, but along those lines. The front aspect was of a flat, shovel-nosed device, and the rear was a long tapering deck meeting an upswept curve from the bottom of the rear fenders in a sharp cutoff containing the light clusters. Rearward visibility was nil, top speed was in the same range as Miura, acceleration blinding and the price astronomic. Production was very limited, and individual vehicles tend to differ from each other as gradual alterations were made; the 4.9-liter engine with which the model was introduced was dropped in favor of the 4-liter, NACA ducts were built into the body sides to aid cooling, more ducts were added just behind the cockpit and air intakes built into the tops of the rear fenders. The interior was revised after a while and then even the chassis was redesigned as a tubular item.

Even before the Countach had been announced Lamborghini were building cars which may or may not have been better than Ferraris but were beyond doubt at the very fringe of automobile styling and design. Owning a Lamborghini may well be a satisfying state of affairs. Driving one even more rewarding, but getting one serviced or repaired is somewhat less amusing.

Typical of this was the Marzal, which never got past prototype stage. Designed by Gandini in 1967, it was built by Bertone, a four-seater coupe glazed both above and below the waistline, with gullwing doors, a transverse straight six engine (effectively half of the Lamborghini V12) and which preceded the Countach by several years.

Its production format was the Urraco, at least in body styling, although by then the fully-glazed gullwing door had given way to something rather more conventional. Although body styling of the Urraco was still in the supercar league the interior owed little, if anything, to ergonomics. It looked fine from a distance but was difficult to drive since the principal instrumentation was so widely scattered.

Nevertheless the Urraco was popular in its class, and once again it demonstrated superb handling and overwhelming power which put it in a class beyond the psychological limits of most of the people likely to drive it.

Based on the Urraco came another prototype in 1974 — the Bravo, another Bertone/Gandini project which this time was wedge-shaped, all straight lines and tinted glass. Once again rear vision was non-existent, but in cars which travel at those sort of speeds rearview mirrors or even rear windows do seem to be superfluous. However prototypes are intended to be just that, and road-going considerations do not intrude on the otherwise perfectly smooth design. Unlike most manufacturers Lamborghini, along with a handful of specialists, are able to translate design prototypes into road cars with few apparent changes in appearance. Esoteric, expensive, impractical and temperamental, maybe, but it is the implied prestige of owning a car which is all those things plus stupendously fast which keeps them in business.

Top right: Almost the 'acceptable' face of Lamborghini, possibly the least exotic of the breed, the Uracco S.

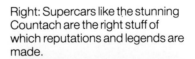

Right: Supercars like the stunning Countach are the right stuff of which reputations and legends are made.

Lotus

The name Lotus is almost as synonymous with motor racing and almost as well-known as its Italian counterpart, Ferrari. Both companies are makers of low-volume specialist sportscars, both are the result of one man's driving ambitions and both exist because in each case that ambition has been directed almost entirely towards motor racing, and the production road cars have been almost a developmental sideline which has paid the rent for the race teams.

Anthony Colin Bruce Chapman was born in Richmond in 1928, began a brief excursion into the second-hand car trade while studying engineering at college and then moved on to motor racing. His first project was a rebuilt 1930 Austin Seven which he converted for trials use. Forced to re-register it he dreamt up an entirely new name for the car and it became Lotus number one. Number two followed after

his service in the RAF, and his cars were so successful that the Lotus Engineering Company was formed in 1952. At first it operated from a stable behind his father's public house, but Chapman's plans extended a great deal further than that.

By the mid-fifties Chapman had designed his own sportscar, a fiberglass body with a 4-ohc Coventry Climax engine. His Elite was the first of the Lotus genre to be aimed at an audience wider than the club racing fraternity which had so far bought Lotus kits for weekend racing, and it was the need to produce this car in bulk which led to his acquisition of the wartime airfield at Hethel in Norfolk, a few miles outside Norwich.

As an engineer Chapman had his own ideas about chassis design and suspension geometry, and Lotus cars swiftly became renowned for their fleetness and incredible handling. At the same time Chapman developed his own way of making the fiberglass bodies which was cost-effective but produced a high quality finish; even today factory tours do not enter that part of the buildings in which the body-molding process is conducted.

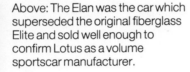

Above: The Elan was the car which superseded the original fiberglass Elite and sold well enough to confirm Lotus as a volume sportscar manufacturer.

Left: Weather protection poor, comfort minimal, luxury zero, the Lotus Seven was the closest thing to a road-going single-seat race car ever made.

Because of the strange taxation methods which existed at the time Lotus cars were offered for many years as kits or complete cars. In truth the kits were fully-assembled cars with little work to be done other than fitting the engine and gearbox, but they were much cheaper in this guise, although the procedure was dropped when the tax laws changed. By that time Lotus had moved on and up, trading especially from the successes of the Formula One team, which relied heavily on Chapman's brilliance as a designer. Lotus were the first race team to use the now-legendary Cosworth DFV, being given its exclusive use for a whole year before it was made available to the rest of the Formula One world and went on to become the most popular and successful Grand Prix engine ever, with more than 150 wins to its credit.

Like Cosworth, Lotus used a Ford base when they began producing their own engines, although their high-performance screamers bore little resemblance to the engines in the family saloons for which they had been designed. For years Lotus road cars relied on a dual ohc version of the Ford 1.6-liter four-cylinder engine before the change to their own powerplant developed in conjunction with Jensen—Healey. Indeed, if Jensen had not participated, it is unlikely that Lotus would have found the financial muscle necessary to develop their own engine.

From the Elite Lotus went on to the Elan, the tremendously good-looking Elan Plus Two, the mid-engined Europa and then the Elite/Eclat range of four-seat GT cars, as well as the current Esprit two-seater. Throughout this the road cars suffered from a quality problem, with irritating faults quickly developing on cars only a few miles old, but the race cars seemed to go from strength to strength in the hands of drivers like Jim Clark, Graham Hill, Jochen Rindt and Emerson Fittipaldi and enjoyed an invincible run with Mario Andretti in 1978.

Throughout the entire period one of the great Lotus success stories was the rudimentary Lotus Seven. Frequently described as an upholstered roller skate without the upholstery, the Seven was the closest thing to a four-wheel motorcycle ever produced. Tiny and cramped, with weather equipment which was little more than a gesture to the elements, the Seven produced the kind of performance and roadholding normally only encountered in full-blown race cars. Powered initially by Ford's four-cylinder engine, the car was fast enough. Later, as Lotus engines became available, these too were applied to the Seven, and the ultimate development of the Ford 1600 crossflow engine, the big-valve 1558 twin-cam, produced maximum horsepower at the rear wheels and maximum impact on the driver. Infinitely forgiving and generally responding happily to frightening applications of power, the Seven could be hurled around race tracks or country lanes with almost nonchalant ease. For years it was advertised as the fastest-accelerating production car in the world, but it could also be the most uncomfortable.

When the tax laws affecting kits changed, and Lotus moved upmarket, production of the Seven ceased because factory space was needed for other cars and in any case the image was all wrong. Demand for the car refused to abate, however, and one of the largest dealers in Lotus Sevens bought the tooling and the rights, and the car continues in production today, built by Caterham Car Sales, known as the Caterham Seven, every bit as basic and still displaying shattering speed and agility. There is, of course, a waiting list for new models, and second-hand examples maintain an extremely high price.

Mercedes

Karl Benz began his working life in 1864 as a locksmith, but soon moved to a steam locomotive works. His ideas for the development of a two-stroke engine led him to set up in business on his own and by 1884 the two-stroke was running adequately with coil ignition while everybody else was still experimenting with hot tube ignition. He followed Nikolaus Otto's example with the four-stroke engine soon after and by 1886 his tricycle was in frequent use. A four-wheeler followed by 1892, but Benz was slow to follow other developments and at first turned his back on pneumatic tires and in-line four-cylinder engines. He was left a little behind as a result, while other pioneers like Gottlieb Daimler prospered. Daimler produced what was probably the first successful four-wheel car, based on a converted horse-drawn carriage, in 1886, and began supplying cars to assorted gentry. One of these, Emile Jellinek, bought 36 early Daimlers for distribution across Europe and France on the strict understanding that he could call them after his daughter, Mercedes. These first cars to bear the Mercedes name raced so successfully in 1899 that the Daimler company from then on used the name for all their cars.

A great amount of effort was dedicated to racing and it was here that Daimler and Benz found themselves protagonists, and cars like the legendary Blitzen Benz of 1909 were competing against the Daimler company's 1914 Mercedes Grand Prix. The Great War brought a temporary stop to the rivalry, but racing continued almost as soon as hostilities ceased. Talks of a merger between the two companies first

Left: The Mercedes SSK, introduced in 1928, with supercharged 7.1 liter engine producing some 225bhp thanks to Ferdinand Porsche's ministrations. Below: One of the 4.5-liter Mercedes which took the first three places in the 1914 French Grand Prix.

began in the economic wasteland of 1919, but amalgamation didn't finally take place until 1926, when they became Daimler Benz AG in June of that year. As part of the deal the three-pointed star of Daimler was combined with the Benz circular laurel wreath to form a trademark which would become an almost unequalled symbol of excellence.

And along with excellence came the quest for speed and power; while Daimler Benz continually supplied luxury touring cars of great excellence they also built sports roadsters of extreme performance and good looks, usually based on the bigger cars but designated 'K' (*kurz* – short) for their smaller dimensions. Daimler Benz also perfected the supercharger at this time, and by the late twenties were supplying cars like the 6.8-liter S and the 7.1-liter SS which were delivering anywhere between 160 and 200bhp, giving top speeds of around 100mph, effortless cruising and blinding acceleration. The 1928 SSK is probably the best-remembered vehicle of this type and period.

By the thirties the Daimler Benz team were heavily involved with Grand Prix racing, and the W series cars began to leave their mark in the record books. The supercharged W25 dominated the 1935 GP season with its 430bhp but by 1937 it had been superseded by the enormous 650bhp of the W125, which turned in a top speed of 200mph. Smaller cars with better streamlining followed, and the W154 and 163 had less power than their predecessors but were almost as fast thanks to their smaller frontal area and much higher supercharger boost – around 25lbs as opposed to 10 or 12. The second war, of course, put a stop to all that, and it wasn't until 1948 that production restarted with the 170, but it was the early fifties before the Mercedes name appeared on a string of cars which were indisputably classics in their own right – the sportscar line which began with the roadgoing 300SL.

Derived from the big 300S saloon, the 300SL was a lightweight sportscar which, although not as powerful as its predecessors, at 175bhp, was so reliable that in its first season it made second place on its debut outing at the

Mille Miglia and then won the following four races it was entered for, culminating in the total victory of the three-car Mercedes team at the 1952 Le Mans 24 hours. The factory withdrew from racing the following year, but made the gullwing 300SL available as a roadgoing vehicle, using fuel injection, by Bosch, developed from aero engines, for the first time. Their 3-liter six-cylinder ohc engine gave 215bhp and a top speed of 160mph, the latter largely due to the streamlined shape and low frontal area. Even with all that power on tap the car was still extremely well-mannered,

Right: The 1957 300SC coupe, with more than a hint of elegance from its prewar ancestors.

Left: The best-known and most recognizable Mercedes ever, the 1955 300SL gullwing. Below: Graceful side view of the 300 SL roadster. Below right: A 1964 230SL.

and would pull from around 30mph in top gear, although it ran 0–60mph in 7 seconds or just over.

The 300SL was so successful that it would set the standard for Mercedes roadgoing sportscars for years to come, and its tubby shape would eventually streamline, by degrees, into the super-smooth city slicker which is the present-day two-seat luxury offering from Mercedes. The same parameters which were laid down by the 300SL also still apply; extreme tractability, tremendous power, opulent luxury and superb engineering.

Mercedes returned to the racetrack in 1954 after a short absence; they entered the arena with the 3-liter straight eight W196 GP car, which went well in the hands of people like Fangio and Moss. As the W196 streamliner sportscar it was equally superb and eventually became the 300SLR of 1954/5. It was in 1955, after Levegh's horrific accident, that the Fangio/Moss 300SLR, at the time well in the lead of the Le Mans 24 hours, was withdrawn, and Mercedes withdrew from racing altogether. However the team had established such a reputation that further racing seemed unnecessary.

The 300SL shape carried on through the fifties as a road car, though, but the gullwing doors which had characterized the legend soon passed on in favor of more conventional openings. The last 300SL was made in 1963, by which time it was available as a soft-top roadster and also as a four-cylinder tourer, the 190SL. It was replaced by the rather more angular 230SL, an elegant, wide-based car which, like its sporty forerunners, wore the Mercedes three-pointed star in rather larger proportions than the understated and luxurious saloons. Aside from the emblem, its racebred heritage was apparent in every line of its bodywork, and even the new-generation sportscars, with concessions to safety like their massive wraparound lights visible on every part of their bodywork, could not disguise their parentage.

The 280 series were the follow-up, introduced in 1968, with this new-style bodywork, and were followed in short order, in 1971 by the new V8-engined 350SL, with a wedge-shape body which still harked back to the gullwing 300SL of the mid-fifties but had little of the engineering left unaltered. Years of research using the gullwing C111 had

led to developments in suspension and engineering, all of which began to appear on the production cars, although the C111's flirtation with Wankel engines and turbos failed to materialize on the line, except on the big diesel saloons like the 300SD, which owed much to the turbo diesel versions of C111, which had produced 235bhp and 200mph out of 30lbs boost in 1974. The turbo has yet to make an appearance on the sportscars, but remembering how well Mercedes did with supercharging in the thirties, it is unlikely that the possibilities are being ignored.

All pictures: The superb 500SL, a worthy successor to a long and prestigious lineage.

MG T Series

The MG factory had been doing very well on the racetracks, had been at the forefront of a great deal of engineering design and development, but as the Great Depression eased slowly into the distance Lord Nuffield decreed that what the company needed was a high production rate of small cheap cars. So in 1935, amid howls of protest, he closed down all racing activities and redirected their energies. Cecil Kimber, John Thornley and Hubert Charles scrounged Nuffield parts and attached them to a small two-seat sportscar which contained mostly Morris parts. It was an MG Midget, the TA, first of a series of cars which would remain in production for the next twenty years and would earn places in record books, race result-sheets and the hearts of thousands of owners.

Practically every one of the T-series MGs offended rather than pleased the enthusiasts when it was launched, before being accepted into the fold, and the TA was no exception. It wasn't a race car, didn't have overhead camshaft layout but traditional pushrods, and was cluttered with 'unnecessary' equipment like air cleaner, thermostat and belt-drive dynamo to which racing MG afficianados were totally unused. But its brief was to appeal to the everyday motorist, to sell and to make money, which it fulfilled more than

adequately. In fact it fulfilled it so well that the TA was still in production at the outbreak of the 1939 war, which was unusual in an era when motor manufacturers felt obliged to produce a new model each year.

It was a basic two-seat convertible powered by a 1292cc engine originally designed for a saloon car, and the steel panels of the body were tacked to a wooden frame which was in turn bolted to the chassis. Although it was a convertible it was designed to be driven with the roof down, and even the flat windshield folded forwards to aid visibility. The wooden spoked steering wheel adjusted for rake; there was a large speedometer and equally large rev counter which were illuminated for night driving. It had a map light inside and fog light outside and the doors even had handles inside and out. It was exceptionally well equipped by comparison to previous MGs and other cars of the period.

The car was an enormous success and carried the factory through the boom years up to 1939. Almost at the very moment war was declared its successor, the TB, was introduced, after the TA had sold 3000 units. From the outside there was little or no discernible difference between the TA and the TB, the most obvious being the positioning of the spokes on the wheels. The big change was the engine. Owners had complained that the TA couldn't be tuned, and the TB was the first to be fitted with the XPAG engine, which remained with the T series for the next 15 years. Slightly smaller, at 1250cc, it was stronger, more reliable, revved harder, produced more power in stock trim, and could easily be tuned to give even greater power outputs.

Above and right: Details from the first of a successful and popular line, the MG TA.

Below: Honorable ancestor to the T series, this is a PB.

Left: Introduced in 1949, the TD was the most popular of the T series cars despite initial resistance from purists. Below: Following the 1947 Nuffield edict – export or die – came major efforts to secure overseas markets, like this TD in export trim.

But timing of the new model launch was all wrong; MG made only slightly more than 300 before the outbreak of war and the factory was turned over to essential work. Sportscar production was suspended for the duration, but when it resumed the TB was brought back to the production lines with a few very minor changes. It was rechristened the TC, and it was this model which gained the T series cars the universal approval of enthusiasts everywhere. A great part of the philosophy behind the TC was a determination to export in large numbers and the TC therefore showed distinct signs of some serious market research. Perhaps the single most obvious change was made because of the American demand for more elbow room in their cars, and the TC was thus some three inches wider inside than the TB. Electrical equipment was updated as well, and the two six-volt batteries hidden under the luggage floor were replaced by one twelve-volt battery in the engine compartment.

In this form the TC was a winner. Some 3000 TAs had been made in the four years before the war; 10,000 TCs were made in the four years following it, before the introduction of the most popular T series of them all, the TD. This was very different in appearance to its three predecessors although the method of construction remained the same – steel panels on ash framework – but it was lower and sleeker than before. What really upset the enthusiasts, at least to begin with – was the addition of steel bumpers for the first time and the loss of the spoked wheels, replaced now by fifteen-inch pressed steel items. Purists protested, but eventually got over their shock, especially as other changes included independent front suspension and rack-and-

pinion steering, which improved the car's behavior no end. A new chassis and new rubber mountings for the gearbox improved the ride as well. The TD was a rather civilized sportscar.

Despite the initial dislike it sold well, the American market liking it particularly. In four years the TD ran to slightly less than 30,000 units, a considerable advance over the TC's 10,000. During the four years only minor changes were made to the car, the most important being the arrival of the uprated 57bhp engine after about 9000 units had been built. The body changed not at all, and in any case was only slightly different to its predecessors, but the next model in the series, the TF of 1953, was changed considerably; radically changed in the eyes of the enthusiasts, and naturally opinion of the time inclined to the belief that it had changed for the worse.

The changes had been effected mostly by a loss of height around the scuttle, a cut in the height of the radiator as well as a slanted installation and by mounting the headlamps directly into the fenders. Overall, the car was about an inch lower than the TD and altogether sleeker. Enthusiasts hated it. The new shape gave it a much smaller frontal area, though, and with no other modifications it was faster than the TD. After about 10,000 units the XPAG engine was finally laid to rest, and replaced by the 1500cc XPEG which BMC had just developed for the Magnette saloons — the 3400 vehicles fitted with this engine were faster — capable of about 90mph — than the 1250 versions, for very little penalty of increased fuel consumption.

The demise of the TF was swift, almost sudden. In production only from October 1953 to May 1955, 9600 were made in eighteen months before the new-shape MGA replaced it and went on to compete in a sportscar market which now included the Jaguar XK and the Healey 3000, whose body design was far more up-to-date and heavily influenced the MGA. In 19 years (13 if you discount the war period) the T series had run through five different body types and a total of 52,649 of them had been produced. Those which survive today are indisputably collectors' items; real sportscars in a classic mold. To prove it, great numbers of them, all five different variants, are still involved in very serious racetrack competition, not only against each other or at 'classic' events, but in the everyday hurly-burly of circuit racing and hillclimb.

Left and top left: The YB saloon, produced between 1947 and 1953, owed many components to the T, including the 1250cc engine.

Right and above: The TF was launched in 1955 to howls of protest from existing fans of the T series, most of whom hated it at once. It was described at the time as being a TD with its face pushed in.

Left: 1933 V12 Packard Dietrich.
Below: 1930 Packard 7-34
Speedster.

Packard

Packard was one of the few motor companies supplying luxury limousines to survive the Depression without the backup of large corporate finance like that which Cadillac were able to call upon. Instead the company saw and recognized the threat, downgraded their range and tooled up for volume production, introducing the straight eight 120 in 1935 at less than $1000. Within two years they had produced a six-cylinder version of the same model which was even cheaper, and production soared from around 6000 cars in 1934 to over 100,000 in 1937.

The six-cylinder model, now called the 110, was available in several versions, but the best-remembered car of the period was the convertible 120 designed by Darrin, now accorded classic status by the Classic Car Club of America.

It was a sporty roadster with raked windshield and cut-down doors, powered by a 282 straight eight, and was the flagship of a series which restored Packard's pre-slump fortunes. Their tiny production figure of 1934 had been well down on previous efforts — production had risen above 50,000 as long ago as 1928 with the introduction of the fifth series of the six-cylinder convertible coupés and the sixth Series Eight. It was the eights which really gave Packard the selling power, however, and for some years afterwards the company remained committed to an eight-cylinders-only policy, all of which carried Samuel Packard's personal emblem on their grille — a pelican.

The seventh Series Eight was introduced in the summer of 1929, confirming Packard as a manufacturer of luxury saloons which were considered impressive enough for them to be the official vehicle of a series of Presidents right up to Harry Truman. The reputation was also founded on reliability as well as opulence; in 1931 Prince Eugene of Belgium crossed the Sahara by car, choosing two of the seventh Series Eight as his transport.

Then came the Depression and the subsequent reversal of the company's fortunes by that reversal of marketing strategy, and so Packard arrived at the outbreak of the war with a strong production lineup, still featuring their cheaper sedans, but with a top-line offering of vehicles powered by their now-legendary straight eight and featuring custom-built bodywork by Darrin, Rollston and LeBaron. During the war years Packard built Rolls-Royce engines under license, notably the Merlin which powered aircraft, tanks and PT boats, and emerged from the conflict in a sound financial position when most other independent makers were deep in debt.

In the immediate postwar period the same marketing arrangements which had raised them from the Depression so successfully were continued, but had completely the opposite effect. The cheaper 110 series cars were continued, and achieved little else other than damaging the Packard image. The big eights were still everything they should have been, but body styles between the sixes and eights (both now designated 'Clipper') were identical. Anybody who spent the money on an eight-cylinder car was indistinguishable from a six-cylinder owner, and in a market in which the automobile was an increasingly important sign of prestige this was a serious error. Cadillac left their cheap cars, LaSalle, out of the postwar range and sold everything they could build, while Packard suffered. Very quickly Cadillac replaced them as the most prestigious car on the American road and remained in the number one position from then on.

In the early fifties Packard opted for a reversion to their original ethos and announced that they would alter their range, and once more build only formal, luxury sedans, a stratagem which might have worked for the still-sound company but for the unfortunate purchase of the ailing Studebaker concern in 1954. Nevertheless the '55 Packard was a completely new car, beginning with the replacement of the straight eight by a powerful 320 V8, load-levelling torsion bar suspension and more besides.

But quality was not as it should have been, and although things were much improved by the following year most potential customers had heard sufficient bad reports about the '55 models to discourage them from owning the '56 lookalike. Production for 1956 was down to about 10,000 units, and in August their President, James Nance, resigned as the company was bought up by Curtiss-Wright. They managed to continue production for a while, making 5000 Clippers in 1957 and introducing a four-car range in 1958, but after that the company produced no further vehicles although Curtiss-Wright kept the name alive for a further four years. In 1962 Packard, which had once been the United States' most luxurious make of car, vanished.

Above: The superb 1936 Packard 120 16 series convertible.

Left: The 1949 Super 8 Deluxe Saloon.

Porsche

In most areas of automobile design, engineering and construction Ferdinand Porsche is recognized as a genius. His first connection with cars was a design engineer, and he had a hand in many of the products which came from some of the greatest names in car manufacture — Daimler, Mercedes-Benz, Steyr, NSU and Auto-Union are a few — but his own name didn't appear on any car until 1948, two years after the establishment of the Porsche design company in Austria. Right from the very start — in fact since the early thirties when he had talked the Hitler government into funding three sports racing cars — Porsche was interested only in sportscars, which may seem strange for a man who was 72 when he finally founded his own company to build them. But it was engineering excellence which was his only goal, and the perfection of engineering which is required to produce reliable racing hardware was his major challenge. He lived just long enough to see his first serious race car, the Volkswagen-based 356 win its class at Le Mans in 1951 before succumbing to a stroke the following year.

His son Ferry took over where he left off, and the Porsche

Above left: Interior of the famed 356. Above: Rear end of the 356B Roadster with that rarity of convertible motoring, an effective and well-fitted hood. Below: The exceptionally clean design of the 356, with rounded shape so unusual in other cars of the period.

factory has never concerned itself with anything but sports racing cars, using the world's classic races as a testbed and, by virtue of a series of Porsche processions to the chequered flag, almost a marketing exercise as well. Everything which has been learned on the racetrack has in some way been used to the advantage of the road cars, and although Porsche have recently been producing front-engine, watercooled cars the legend was based on the VW-based rear-mounted flat fours and sixes and on a car which has changed only slightly since the introduction of the 356 more than thirty years ago. Now a supercar in its own right, the 911 owes its engineering and appearance to that first sportscar.

On the road the 356 and the Speedster were the cars which dominated the fifties. Built out of a spaceframe chassis, they used mostly existing VW parts, including a modified 1131cc flat four which gave some 60bhp by virtue of cylinder head modification. The engine was fitted backwards – with the transmission to the front – in order to keep as much weight as possible within the wheelbase, and the VW's torsion bar rear suspension was also fitted backwards. The 356/2 was the follow-up, and this went back to Porsche's original layout for the Beetle: platform chassis, engine and suspension the right way round and a little concession to space. The engine had reached the end of its development life, and Porsche introduced a 1500cc option which, fitted to the Speedster, helped to make the Porsche name as important to sportscars as any other no matter how long-established. The Speedster was an immediate success, particularly in America, and more than 5000 of them were made in the first year of production, 1954/5.

At about the same time the factory produced the 550, which was the first of the marque to be designed specially for racing and they began what was an impressive series of class wins in 1954, taking Le Mans in that year and again in '55 and '56. It was then that one of their best-known race cars, the RSK, made its debut and after a less than auspicious start came second to Ferrari in the world sports-car championship in 1958. It was used as a base for Porsche's brief foray into Formula 1 and Formula 2 circuit-racing before being developed into the RS60 and then RS61 and its lines were clearly evident in the later 904.

Meanwhile on the road the 356 was still going, although the Speedster was reaching the end of its useful life as it was by now too expensive for the American market. It was replaced by the Speedster D, although America, particularly California, resented the loss of what had by now become their favorite sportscar, and never really took to it. By now though, the 356, in its two-liter, four-camshaft Carrera guise, had established itself as a top-class top-performing sportscar and was but one step away from becoming the all-conquering 911. The curves of the 356 were trimmed away, the doors and windows were larger, and there was more interior space. Space-saving torsion-bar suspension was retained to give the maximum amount of luggage space and the maximum amount of room for rear seat passengers. Most of this development work was carried out by the third generation of the Porsche family to become involved, Ferry's son Ferdinand, widely known as Butzi. It was Ferry who made the most of the engine space at the rear, however, filling it with the replacement for the 356's complex four-cam four-cylinder powerplant.

The new engine was a single cam flat six 2-liter unit which was based on the eight-cylinder racing engine, and

Above: The 924, which broke years of Porsche tradition, becoming the first front-engine watercooled car the factory produced. Below: The clip-roof 911 Targa.

involved extensive use of aluminum to keep weight over the rear wheels to a minimum. Originally designated 901, the car was rechristened 911 before its launch and went into production alongside the 356 from late 1964 onwards until the following year, when the 356 was discontinued. Now without a convertible in the range, Porsche quickly produced the 911 Targa, with a clip-off roof section and a central hoop to provide body stiffness which made a pronounced difference to the side-on appearance of the car.

The new engine was uprated in 1966 to give the 911S 160bhp instead of 130, and then the 911T gave the basic package a slightly downmarket approach for the cost-conscious, and the 912 (a 911 with the old 1600 engine) completed the four-car range, all of which were available as fixed-head or Targa for road use. On the racetrack it was a story of more development and more winning, as the 911 went up to 2300cc and then grew fuel injection. The

injection model was sold as a road car in the USA, designated 911E and described as a 2.4-liter car to make the most of Porsche racing success which at the time depended on a 2.4-liter powerplant. But the new Carrera was just around the corner, and in 1973 it appeared, or 500 of them did. Lightweight homologation specials, they carried a 2.7-liter version of the flat six engine which was so successful that by 1974 it was fitted to all of the range except the Carrera RSR, which was given a 200bhp 3-liter version. 1974 was also the year of the G-series 911, fitted with the 5mph impact-absorbing bumpers which were about to become necessary in America and which the squat little body absorbed commendably well, even looking better for it as Porsche yet again turned necessity into a virtue.

Late 1974 also saw what most people accept as the ultimate development of the 911, 25 years after Porsche had set about the manufacture of sports racing cars. It was so

refined and so much better than the run-of-the-mill 911 that the factory christened it the 930. To most people, though, it looked like a 911, and is still thought of as such. And although the engineering was vastly different, the concept and the philosophy were much as they had been with the first 356.

Basically the 930 was little more than a turbocharged three-liter Carrera RSR, although development of the KKK turbocharger had taken years and both clutch and transmission had been strengthened to cope with an engine which now delivered 300bhp. And every one of those horsepower was being used, as the 930 shot from 0–60mph in 5.3 seconds, passed the standing quarter in 13.4 seconds and went all the way to its top speed of more than 160mph. All of this was coupled with the world-renowned Porsche handling, and all of it was attached to a road car. On the track the 930 was even hotter.

Below: A full view of one of the most attractive cars ever made, the awesome Porsche 930. Above: The intercooler engine which produces the power to fuel the reputation.

Rolls-Royce

The historic meeting between Charles Rolls and Henry Royce culminated in the signing of an agreement between the two whereby CS Rolls and Company agreed to accept the entire output of Henry Royce Ltd. One was an engineering company, the other a newly-started manufacturer of cars. Both applied stringent standards of quality to their products. They remained as separate companies with a mutual interest for about two years, until in March 1906 they agreed to sell their cars under the name of Rolls-Royce for the first time.

Six months later, in September 1906, Charles Rolls made his first sales trip to America, taking with him three cars. One was sold almost immediately – to a Texan, of course – one was retained as a demonstrator, and the third was put on display at the New York Auto Show in December, where it won four orders for new cars. A distributor was appointed, W C Martin, of New York City, and in the following year he placed orders for a further 17 cars, one of the first going to Mrs Astor, the trend-setting leader of New York Society. Sales of Rolls-Royce cars didn't really pick up for some years, however, after the Brewster coachbuilding firm took over the distributorship in 1914, selling about 100 vehicles before the outbreak of war.

In 1919 Rolls-Royce again set about capturing the American market, which they regarded as being more lucrative than their own domestic potential. Import restrictions meant that in order to be competitive they would have to establish a manufacturing facility in the USA, and accordingly a factory was purchased from the Springfield Wire Wheel Company at Springfield, Mass. Manufacturing was set up under the guidance of F Henry Royce, and the locally-recruited workforce was strengthened by the arrival of 53 foremen and supervisors from the Derby factory, who emigrated with their families. In 1920 it was announced that production was about to commence at Springfield and that the American-made cars would be the equal of those built in Derby.

It made sense, however, to use locally-available parts, if only to ensure continuity of servicing and repairs, and slowly the number of imported components began to

Above: 1922 Springfield Silver Ghost Tourer by Rolls-Royce Custom Coachwork. This terminology covered a number of designs which were built by local firms to the order of Rolls-Royce of America Inc. Below: 1921 Silver Ghost Albany dual-cowl Phaeton.

Left and above: 1925 Springfield Silver Ghost Stratford convertible coupe by Brewster. Rolls-Royce bought out the prestigious Brewster coachbuilding company in 1925.

dwindle so that when production began in 1921 only the first 25 chassis were identical to the Derby item. The early Springfield cars are plated 'Rolls-Royce Custom Coachwork', which meant only that they were designed by Rolls-Royce; the bodies were built by a variety of coachbuilders like Willoughby, Merrimac or Smith Springfield. Later, in 1923, Rolls-Royce America set up its own coachworks department in Springfield and kept the work in house, but it still didn't stop them from building the most expensive automobiles available in America; top of the range was the Mayfair Cabriolet, which carried an ex-works sticker price of $15,880, some $4000 more than the next most expensive domestic product and considerably removed from Ford's cheapest Model T ($260).

This huge price reflected the recent conversion at Springfield, in 1924, to the production of left-hand-drive cars, leaving the right-hand-drive cars as something of a burden to the salesmen, and which had necessitated some changes to steering linkages and other parts. And Rolls-Royce of America experienced considerable – cheaper – competition from the comparatively high number of manufacturers who were producing limousines for the luxury end of the market. However in 1925 the Brewster coachbuilding company got into financial trouble and were bought up by Rolls-Royce, bringing one of the prestige American names into the fold, and more and more of the Springfield cars were bodied by them, mostly in designs created by John Inskip.

Despite the competition the twenties were very good years for Rolls-Royce, and the Springfield works produced about 350 vehicles each year up until 1932, when the story took a downward turn. This was partly due to the announcement of a new model in England a whole year before it was available in America, causing demand to drop in anticipation, and also, of course, to the Depression. When the new car finally became available from Springfield it incorporated several developments which would only become standard on the Derby cars later on – central chassis lubrication and thermostatic radiator vents for example – but even so Springfield were obliged to import 100 Phantoms from England to meet sales requirements.

All of which conspired to make the Springfield Phantom even more expensive than it had already been, so that by

1929 the Trouville Town Car cost $19,965, a price which was current just as the American factory was dealt another severe, eventually fatal, blow. The introduction of the Phantom II at Derby was even more critical than had been the Phantom I, since it was in every way more of a new car than the previous model. In fact it was so different that Springfield estimated the cost of retooling at about $1 million; coming on top of what had been increasingly leaner years, with sales steadily falling off, it was decided that the price was simply too high, and they relinquished their manufacturing license. They continued to assemble the vehicles which were going through the factory at the time, and the last of these 200 or so cars was delivered in 1935. At the same time Derby built 125 left-hand-drive Phantom IIs, 116 of which were sent to America to be bodied at Springfield, and among these were some of the most elegant vehicles which the factory there had ever produced – the Henley, Newport and Newmarket among them – a fitting close to an era of graceful and good-looking car production.

As that period gradually wound down the name of the company was changed to the Springfield Manufacturing Corporation, and a year later, in 1935, they filed for bankruptcy. In 1936 all of the company's assets apart from the Springfield factory itself were sold to rivals Pierce-Arrow, which followed them into the bankruptcy court a scant two years later.

John Inskip kept the Springfield spirit alive for some while, taking over part of the Brewster building and putting his own individualistic bodies on some 20 Phantom chassis between 1936 and 1945 as well as on chassis of various other manufacturers. At the same time Brewsters were coach-building their own brand of excellence for customers who couldn't afford Rolls-Royce but still required an above-average measure of style. Almost exclusively they used a stretched Ford chassis for this purpose.

The war put an almost complete stop to all this activity, and although a few of these fine cars surfaced in the immediate postwar days they were sold for a pittance which belied their former glory, a sad end to a company whose cars, while perhaps not in the true traditions of their rather staid parent in Derby, were superbly engineered and bore a certain air of flamboyance which the British cars lacked. This is more than borne out by a brief glance at the Springfield order book; along with America's wealthiest families – Astor, Carnegie, Vanderbilt, Guggenheim and Rockefeller were a few – most of Hollywood's leading lights were also represented – Daryl Zanuck, Tom Mix, Al Jolson, Clara Bow, Norma Talmadge, Zeppo Marx, Pola Negri, Gloria Swanson and Mack Sennett were all there, which must say something about their good taste as well as about the quality of the product. Today Rolls-Royce retains its aura of quality and exclusivity.

Right and below: 1929 Phantom 1 Sedan, originally built by Park Ward with fabric coachwork, but rebodied by Brewster as a Huntingdon Sedan.

Above: A mixture of AC expertise, Ford power and the Shelby magic, the Cobra paid lip-service only to driver comfort, and was built for the race track. Below: In the year the 427 Cobras first appeared the popular option was still the 289, like this '66.

Shelby American

Carroll Hall Shelby was a racing driver first and foremost. He'd driven for Porsche, won Le Mans in 1959 for Aston Martin — and then been forced to retire because of a heart condition. In order to keep in touch with his first love, motor racing, he decided to build cars for other people to race. He approached Ford for backing, with the idea of building a Ford sportscar and he couldn't have chosen a better moment, since America was just embarking upon what would later be called the musclecar era and Ford were without a contender.

The result, as history shows, was the Cobra. Produced by AC Cars at Thames Ditton in England, the Cobra was powered originally by Ford's new 221 V8. The prototype was built at Dean Moon's premises in California and appeared on the cover of assorted motoring magazines painted a variety of different colors in order to create the impression that the Cobra was enjoying a huge production run.

In fact the reverse was true, and the few cars which were built were almost all different from each other. In any case each time an improvement to the model was announced many existing owners brought their Cobras back to the factory to have them updated. So it was that when the Cobra began to be fitted with the larger 289 V8 many of the first 75, fitted with a 221 bored up to 260, were brought back for transplants.

Shelby's aim in all this was simply to build a race car which would win. Cobra's first race outing in late 1962 was at Riverside, and Billy Krause had a lead of more than a mile when a stub axle broke and the car retired, but the potential had been proved. In 1965 Craig Breedlove, then land speed record holder, took a Cobra to the Bonneville Oval and established 23 new national and international records, and at the end of the year Shelby withdrew the Cobras from competition, after they had captured the USA's first and only FIA World Manufacturers Championship for GT cars.

Ford, who by 1966 were committed to their Total Performance package, were not quite as enthusiastic about the Cobras as they might have been. Although through them the Ford V8 had gained entry to just about every winner's circle which mattered there were two drawbacks. Le Mans so far remained unconquered and in any case the Cobras were noticeably a Shelby product rather than Ford. Shelby was well aware of this, and it was one of the reasons he held the new 427 Cobras back from race involvement since it would almost certainly have outshone Ford's own Le Mans contender, the GT40. In any case there was little likelihood of Shelby ever producing the minimum 100 cars a year necessary for the 427 Cobra to gain homologation. What happened instead was that the factory built all-out race cars which were then given the minimum of niceties to make them street legal.

However the GT 40 was initially rather disappointing to Ford, and failed to live up to expectations, so eventually the

whole GT program was handed over to Shelby, with immediate and almost miraculous results. The GT 40 won at Le Mans two successive years, gaining a 1-2-3 whitewash in 1966. And as part of the GT program, Shelby released the Shelby Mustang GT 350 in 1965. Like the Cobras, very few GT 350s are like any other GT 350; if the production line ran short of any items then cars were simply produced without them, and two vehicles with consecutive chassis numbers could have completely different trim specifications.

The basic cars came with a Shelby-prepared Ford 289 with hi-rise manifold, four bbl carburetor, four-speed box, limited slip differential, ventilated front disks and a whole list of chassis tuning work and/or extras which reduced the Mustang's well-known understeering character to an almost neutrally balanced ride. The specification list was long and detailed, right down to the identification flash for the bodywork, but as Ford themselves had learned, the extras and alterations were only part of the story. Each car was individually built and each car benefitted from the special attentions of Shelby and his team of mechanics; without that magic touch there was still something missing which all the extras in the world couldn't replace.

Even so the dispassionate hand of accountancy began to interfere as Ford urged Shelby to conform to normal profit margins. Efficiency experts from Ford forced the abandon-ment of the more time-consuming modifications during the 1966 model year, and gradually the cars began to lose character and charisma. Ford were now heavily involved with product identification, and 1967 saw the end of the Cobra since Ford were more interested in hot Mustangs.

But the introduction of the new-shape Mustang in 1967 heralded the end of the Shelby cars. The new model was far too big and heavy to respond to the Shelby performance criteria and became instead more of a four-seat GT saloon — until the 428ci GT 500. This was an absolute brute of a car which, it was rumored, could destroy a set of rear tires in an evening, but came with power steering, automatic trans-mission and, occasionally, airconditioning, which left them a far luxurious cry from the original GT 350.

The era of the performance car was ending. Fuel crises and environmental considerations were bringing the high-horsepower cars to a halt. The Shelby Mustangs were frequently sold with their power output way underquoted, just to help owners get insurance. Along with the Road-runner, the Shelbys were among the most crashed cars available, purely because of their awesome power, some-thing which was now becoming to be regarded as decidedly antisocial. In 1969 Shelby closed down production, and the last few hundred cars were given an almost valedictory special paintjob and sold as 1970 models.

All pictures: Top of the range as far as driver comfort is concerned and with enough power to satisfy all but the most committed race driver, the GT 500.

Studebaker

The Studebaker Corporation had been building horse-drawn vehicles since 1852 and built its first car in 1902. In the late twenties the firm encountered severe financial problems after the failure of their low-priced model for the lean years, the Erskine. The 1929 Crash damaged them again, and in the opening years of the thirties they had another failure with the ill-starred Rockne, finally going into receivership in 1933.

Rescued by Paul Hoffman and Harold Vance, Studebaker gradually improved until by the 1939 introduction of the good-looking and economical Champion their fortunes were fully restored as production rose above 100,000 for the first time since 1929, and they became eighth-largest manufacturer in 1942, the year the war put a stop to civilian car production.

By a combination of good fortune and good planning the postwar Studebaker range represented a considerable facelift on prewar models and was also the first to be announced by a large manufacturer. Largely the product of Virgil Exner, the new Studebakers were so far in advance of contemporary styling that the initial postwar designs remained virtually unchanged for five years, getting yet another revolutionary facelift in 1952 when the 'bullet-nose' style appeared. But the Studebaker plant at South Bend, Indiana, was outdated, underproductive and far removed from the center of the motor industry. As the Studebaker Corporation passed through its centenary year and beyond, the succession of price wars resulting from the Ford vs Chevrolet struggle for market supremacy began to slowly wipe out the uncompetitive independents.

The 1954 merger with Packard served to do little beyond encumbering the new parent company with all the troubles which had beset Studebaker themselves and ensured the eventual demise of Packard. The Curtiss-Wright Corporation, which bought out Studebaker-Packard, let Packard die, but kept Studebaker alive for more than a decade.

1956 saw the advent of several classic models from the Loewy team which had put Studebaker styling so far ahead since the war. Sportiest of these was the new Golden Hawk, a hardtop which shared the same market as Ford's Thunderbird and Chevrolet's Corvette. With the Packard 352 V8 the Hawk should have been competitive – it cost $3061, compared to Corvette's $3149. But even Corvette was in some difficulty, only being reprieved from the accountants' red pens on the introduction of the Thunderbird, so it is unlikely that the Golden Hawk can have made very much of a contribution to Studebaker's financial stability. In any case Studebaker's total production for the year was around 70,000 vehicles while Chevrolet turned out well in excess of two million.

As Packard slowly faded away Studebaker continued; the '57–'58 Golden Hawk dispensed with the heavy Packard 352, replacing it with a blown 289 which produced similar horsepower to the Packard but improved handling thanks to its lower weight. The Hawk range was trimmed down all round as well; the Sky Hawk, Power Hawk and Flight Hawk were all replaced by the Silver Hawk, basically a cheaper, unblown version of the Golden Hawk. These two vehicles were both fine GT cars in the true sense of the word,

carrying passengers rapidly and comfortably over long distances. Like all cars of the type they had a somewhat limited appeal, tending to sell in the enthusiast's end of the market.

Produced by one of the larger combines, Golden Hawk may well have carried on, as did Corvette and Thunderbird, long enough to have established itself as a truly classic vehicle. As part of the Studebaker Corporation it was already doomed. Production figures in 1957 made a total of 74,738 cars. 15,000 of them were Silver Hawk and 4000 Golden Hawk, but by the following year the total had almost halved to around 40,000 and this time Silver Hawk accounted for 7000 vehicles, Golden Hawk a mere 878. That was the last year the Golden Hawk was seen.

Studebaker's fortunes were carried by the Lark series (introduced in 1959) and the Silver Hawk (which became plain old Hawk in 1960) for a few more years, the Lark producing a brief upturn in fortunes in the early sixties. As production began to slide back the last of the Hawks, the Gran Turismo Hawk, was built in 1964. It's replacement, the Corvette-challenging fiberglass Avanti, was late into production and failed to live up to the company's hopes. In 1969 South Bend closed, and Studebaker withdrew all operations to their Hamilton, Ontario plant, where they planned to build 20,000 units per year. An almost total lack of facilities beyond simple production-line work meant that the Hamilton plant was not good enough for a car manufacturer to remain competitive in a high technology field, and Studebaker built their last car in 1966. The Avanti, taken over by two Studebaker dealers in South Bend, continues in production, fitted with a Corvette V8 engine.

Above: The 1954 Starlight Coupe, neat, but without the elegance which characterized the later Hawk series.

Right: 1958 Silver Hawk two-door coupe.

Index

Page numbers in italics refer to illustrations

Acknowledgments

The author and the publisher would like to thank Nicky Wright for supplying the bulk of the photographs in this book. In addition, they are grateful to the following for providing photographs as listed below:

John Adams 16, 16-17, 17, 18, 19 (two), 23
Henry Austin Clark jnr. 42-43
Fotoccompli 94
Andrew Morland 6 (three), 7, 24 (three), 40 (two), 40-41, 54, 55, 56, 88